HEALTHY, WEALTHY, AND WISE

American Enterprise Institute
for Public Policy Research

The American Enterprise Institute sponsors original research on the world economy, U.S. foreign policy and international security, and domestic political and social issues. AEI is dedicated to preserving and strengthening the foundations of a free society—limited government, competitive private enterprise, vital cultural and political institutions, and vigilant defense—through rigorous inquiry, debate, and writing.

The Hoover Institution

The Hoover Institution on War, Revolution and Peace, Stanford University, is a public policy research center devoted to advanced study of politics, economics, and political economy—both domestic and foreign—as well as international affairs. With its world-renowned group of scholars and ongoing programs of policy-oriented research, the Hoover Institution puts its accumulated knowledge to work as a prominent contributor to the world marketplace of ideas defining a free society.

HEALTHY, WEALTHY, AND WISE
Five Steps to a Better Health Care System

John F. Cogan, R. Glenn Hubbard,
and Daniel P. Kessler

THE AEI PRESS
Publisher for the American Enterprise Institute
Washington, D.C.

and

THE HOOVER INSTITUTION
Stanford University
Stanford, Calif.

Available in the United States from the AEI Press, c/o Client Distribution Services, 193 Edwards Drive, Jackson, TN 38301. To order, call toll free: 1-800-343-4499. Distributed outside the United States by arrangement with Eurospan, 3 Henrietta Street, London WC2E 8LU, England.

Library of Congress Cataloging-in-Publication Data
Cogan, John F.
  Healthy, wealthy, and wise : five steps to a better health care system / John F. Cogan, R. Glenn Hubbard, and Daniel P. Kessler.
    p. cm.
Includes bibliographical references and index.
  ISBN 0-8447-7178-3 (cloth: alk. paper)
  1. Health care reform—United States. 2. Medical care, Cost of—United States. 3. Health services accessibility—United States. 4. Insurance, Health—United States. 5. Tax credits—United States. I. Hubbard, R. Glenn. II. Kessler, Daniel P. III. Title.
  [DNLM: 1. Health Care Reform—United States. 2. Health Care Costs—United States. 3. Health Services Accessibility—United States. 4. Insurance, Health—United States. 5. Malpractice—United States. 6. Taxes—economics—United States. WA 540 AA1 C63h 2005]

  RA395.A3C633 2005
  362.1'0425—dc22

                                                    2005019533

  10 09 08 07 06 05   1 2 3 4 5 6

Printed in the United States of America

Contents

Acknowledgments

We are grateful to the Foundation for Better Health for generous financial support; to Joe Antos, Chris DeMuth, Doug Holtz-Eakin, Al Hubbard, Ben Lytle, Cindy Miller, Sam Nussbaum, Mark Pauly, Dhan Shapurji, Marc Sumerlin, and Janet Stokes Trantwein for helpful comments and discussions; to Evan Lodes for exceptional research assistance; and to Sam Thernstrom for excellent editorial advice.

Introduction

Health care in the United States has made remarkable advances over the past forty years. Dramatic improvements in medical technology have expanded both the length and quality of life. In general, Americans are remarkably satisfied with the quality of their health care. Yet our health-care system also has several well-known problems: high costs, significant rates of uninsurance, and glaring gaps in quality and efficiency.

How can we preserve the strengths of this system while addressing its weaknesses? Policymakers, like Americans as a whole, are divided about whether we should make private markets work better or increase the government's involvement in health care. Supporters of private markets point out that competition and choice provide consumer satisfaction in most markets; health care should be no different. Supporters of public intervention argue that high costs and imperfect information give government a direct role in health care.

In our view, the unintended consequences of a handful of public policies are in large part responsible for the problems of the health-care system. These policies share a common feature: They fail to promote the proper functioning of markets. In two areas, tax policy and health-insurance regulation, government policy has actively hindered the operation of markets for health services.

Current tax policy generally allows people to deduct employer-provided health-insurance expenditures, but requires direct out-of-pocket medical spending to come from after-tax income. This tax preference has given consumers the incentive to purchase health care through low-deductible, low-copayment insurance instead of paying for it out-of-pocket. This type of insurance has led to today's U.S. health-care market, in which cost unconsciousness and wasteful medical practices are the norm. State health-insurance regulation, by requiring insurers to cover certain types of care and restricting their ability to set premiums, has raised insurance costs and limited the available range of insurance options. These inefficiencies have been an important factor contributing to the rising number of uninsured people.

In three other areas—the provision of health-care information, the enforcement of antitrust laws, and medical malpractice rules—government policy has failed to promote adequately the proper functioning of health-care markets. As a general rule, markets work well when information about product and service prices and quality is widely available. Although recently the federal government has taken steps to disseminate information about health-care prices and quality to both consumers and providers, much more needs to be done to ensure that health-care markets perform their essential role of promoting lower cost and higher quality.

Markets also work well when vigorous competition among suppliers prevails. Government enforcement of anti-trust laws in health-care markets has been too lax. As a consequence, health-care providers are able to engage in anti-competitive practices that drive up prices and reduce quality.

Finally, markets work well when appropriate penalties are levied on suppliers of deficient products and negligent service providers. Current medical malpractice law imposes excessive penalties that have led to costly defensive practices and higher rates of medical errors.

The first step in solving the problems of the U.S. health system must include changing these policies.

In this book, we propose five reforms to improve the ability of markets to create a lower-cost, higher-quality health-care system that is responsive to the needs of individuals. These reforms are summarized in box 1:

1. *Tax reform*: We propose three changes to the tax code, designed to reduce the distorting role of third-party payers, encourage saving for future health-care needs, and reduce the rate of uninsurance.

2. *Insurance reform*: We propose allowing insurance companies to offer health plans on a nationwide basis, free from costly state benefit mandates and excessive rate regulation, to foster more portable, more affordable health

insurance. We also propose a subsidy for persistently high-cost individuals.

3. *Improved provision of information*: We propose public/private partnerships to provide better information to doctors and patients.

4. *Enhanced competition*: We propose greater federal scrutiny of anticompetitive behavior by hospitals and other health-care providers and stricter application of antitrust laws when such behavior is found.

5. *Malpractice reform*: We propose malpractice reform to reduce wasteful treatment and medical errors.

We also propose further study of a sixth reform: revocation or limitation of the current tax preference for nonprofits.

In combination, these reforms will reduce health-care costs by approximately $60 billion per year without reducing the quality of care. These savings will accrue to consumers and workers. Decreases in health spending will lead to decreases in health-insurance costs. And just as increases in health-insurance costs are borne by workers in the form of lower wages, decreases will accrue to them as higher wages.

Cost savings, however, are only one of our goals; our policies will also improve the system's productivity, fairness, and responsiveness. For example, improved health information and malpractice reform will improve quality. Tax reform will make the tax treatment of health expenses more progressive, with the largest gains for low-income households.

Box 1

FIVE STEPS TO A BETTER HEALTH-CARE SYSTEM

1. Health-Care Tax Reform
   - Total deductibility of health-care expenses
   - Expanded health savings accounts
   - Tax credits for low-income individuals and families

2. Insurance Reform
   - Nationwide portable health insurance
   - Subsidized private insurance for the chronically ill

3. Improve Health Information
   - Expand the number and scope of report cards on doctors and hospitals
   - Promote use of "best practices" through guidelines

4. Control Anticompetitive Behavior by Providers and Insurers

5. Reform the Malpractice System

Reducing wasteful spending and inefficient regulation will reduce uninsurance. We estimate that our reforms will provide insurance to at least 6 million—and perhaps as many as 20 million—currently uninsured people. (The wide range of that estimate reflects the considerable uncertainty about the effects of various policies on the uninsured.)

These reforms will also gradually but fundamentally give individuals more control over and choices for their health care. Most notably, tax deductibility and health savings accounts reduce the financial penalty for purchasing medical care directly rather than through employer-provided insurance. Consumers will respond by shifting the type of insurance they purchase to lower-cost catastrophic insurance and away from first-dollar coverage. As the availability of health-care report cards and other user-friendly information devices increases, consumers will become better equipped to make health-care decisions, and as consumers spend less on insurance premiums and more on direct medical-care purchases, health-care providers will become more responsive to their demands than to those of insurance bureaucracies.

Nationwide insurance and reduced mandates will expand the number of insurance choices available. In conjunction with more vigorous enforcement of antitrust laws against health-care providers, this enhanced competition in insurance markets will reduce the cost of insurance for everyone, but likely most for nongroup markets in rural areas where coverage options are currently narrow. Tax credits, by providing additional health-care resources to persons with low and moderate incomes, will make health insurance more financially attractive and broaden their insurance options. As coverage increases and more relatively healthy individuals join health-insurance pools, the range of options will continue to expand, and the cost will decline further.

At the same time, our policies will not abruptly alter the existing system of employer-sponsored health insurance. As we describe below, the tax reforms we propose retain significant incentives for employers to provide health insurance. Our proposed reforms benefit the individual and the employer market alike. We are agnostic about the ultimate balance that should be struck between individual and employer-based insurance; to the extent that they are efficiently able to pool together persons with different health-care risks, employers should continue to provide insurance. However, we firmly believe that this balance should be determined by market forces seeking to deliver the care that individuals want—at the cost they are willing to pay.

Our book proceeds in three chapters. In chapter 1, we outline the challenge facing public policy: retaining and continuing to achieve gains to society from the U.S. health-care system while minimizing its costs, both financial and otherwise. Chapter 2 proposes a market-based approach to accomplishing this goal, explaining why the most important problems with our health-care system are in large part due to five flawed public policies, and showing how five sets of specific reforms can correct these flaws. Chapter 3 quantifies the expected consequences of our reforms, based on estimates of how consumers and providers have responded to past changes in markets for health care, and explains how we calculate their effects on health spending, the uninsured, and the federal budget.

1

The Challenge: Obtaining High-Quality, Affordable Health Care

Everyone agrees that, over the past fifty years, the U.S. health-care system has yielded vast benefits for large numbers of Americans. Yet there are many instances in which today's health care is costly, wasteful, and leaves people without appropriate care. The challenge for public policy is to find a way to keep the (good) sophisticated health-care procedures in instances where they are productive, but avoid the (bad) wasteful spending and its (ugly) relatives—uninsurance, the managed-care backlash, and medical error.

The Good: Innovation

Evidence of the U.S. health-care system's innovative strength is overwhelming. In the 1940s, the discovery of a low-cost process for manufacturing penicillin contributed significantly to the triumph of modern medicine over infectious disease.[1] The Nobel prizes in medicine and physiology have been awarded to more Americans than to researchers in all other countries combined. Eight of the ten most important medical innovations of the past thirty years originated in the United States.[2] Eight of the world's ten top-selling drugs are produced by companies headquartered in the United States.[3]

American consumers recognize the benefits of this system. Survey evidence on this point is clear: 82 percent of Americans are satisfied with the quality of health care they receive; 86 percent are satisfied with their doctors and nurses; and 74 percent rate the quality of hospitals in their area as good or excellent.[4]

The remarkable success we have had in treating cardiovascular disease is a good demonstration of the strengths of our health-care system.[5] Beginning in the 1960s, mortality from cardiovascular disease in the United States began to decline rapidly, falling about 2 percent each year from 1960 to 1995; the cumulative decline over this period was close to two-thirds. To put this dramatic change into context, the decline in mortality from cardiovascular disease explains essentially all of the overall reduction in mortality for the elderly since 1965. For the population as a whole, 98 percent of the reduction in mortality was a result of our progress in fighting cardiovascular disease. There are several causes for this decline in cardiovascular mortality, but evidence indicates that medical care (rather than changes in health behaviors, such as smoking) accounts for a relatively large share of it.[6]

The medical care behind this revolution in cardiovascular health is strongly related to the incentives for innovation in the U.S. system. According to a 2002 study that analyzed the findings of research teams from seventeen different countries, the United States has been one of the leading countries—if not *the* leading country—in promoting the use of intensive medical treatment for serious cardiac disease (see box 2).[7] Generous payments for treatment for heart attack in America led to the early adoption and widespread use of technologically advanced treatments. Countries with weaker incentives for the adoption and implementation of costly technology use these procedures much less.

Were the introduction and diffusion of these costly intensive cardiac procedures in the United States beneficial? On the whole, cost-benefit calculations suggest they were.[8] The typical forty-five-year-old American can expect to have $30,000 spent on his behalf to treat cardiovascular disease over his remaining lifetime. These treatments can be expected to extend this person's life by approximately three years, worth (in economic terms) approximately $120,000. On average, each dollar spent on cardiovascular care generates four dollars' worth of benefits.[9]

New drugs for depression offer another example of the benefits of innovation. Eli Lilly's introduction of Prozac in 1988, followed by the development of several related compounds, revolutionized treatment of this common and debilitating mental illness. These new pharmaceuticals are as effective as their predecessors, are safer and easier to administer, and have fewer adverse side effects, making them more

---

Box 2

THE USE OF CARDIAC PROCEDURES IN NINE COUNTRIES

Countries differ widely in their incentives for, and use of, advanced technological procedures to treat cardiac illness. Some provide weak incentives for adoption and use of technology, including global hospital budgets, capitated or salaried compensation of physicians, and limits on capital equipment purchases. Others provide strong incentives, including generous payments to physicians and hospitals for the provision of additional intensive treatment. Countries also differ in how extensively they use advanced cardiac procedures. For instance, the gold-standard, high-tech diagnostic procedure used to assess artery status is cardiac catheterization or angiography, which may be followed by either coronary artery bypass graft surgery or percutaneous transluminal coronary angioplasty to "revascularize," or remove, arterial blockages.

Figure 1 summarizes the relationship, reported by Mark McClellan and Daniel Kessler, between incentives for the use of these three procedures in 1995 and the

(continued on next page)

---

attractive to both physicians and patients. They are also, however, substantially more expensive than their older, off-patent counterparts. Despite their high cost, the discovery and diffusion of these new pharmaceuticals have been another good health-care investment, with every dollar spent on them returning six to seven dollars in societal benefits.[10]

These two examples illustrate the potential importance to public policy of preserving incentives for innovation in the

(Box 2, *continued*)

FIGURE 1
THE RELATIONSHIP BETWEEN INCENTIVES AND THE USE OF INTENSIVE CARDIAC PROCEDURES

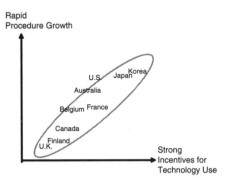

SOURCE: Mark McClellan and Daniel Kessler, eds., *A Global Analysis of Technological Change in Health Care: Heart Attack* (Ann Arbor: University of Michigan Press, 2002).

growth in their use from 1991 to 1995.[11] As figure 1 shows, there is a strong relationship between incentives and procedure growth. Japan and Korea have the strongest incentives for intensive cardiac procedures and the fastest rate of growth. Although pure fee-for-service reimbursement of health-care expenses is rarer in the United States and Australia, significant private financing for health services and a lack of formal constraints on hospitals' use of new technologies have led to very rapid growth in procedure use in those countries as well. France, Belgium, and some Canadian provinces have intermediate incentives and intermediate growth rates; Finland, the United Kingdom, and other Canadian provinces have more limited incentives and the slowest growth in procedure use.

U.S. system. At least for cardiac and mental health care, no one would like to turn back the medical-care clock to the 1950s, even if it meant that they could spend the money they saved on something else.

The Bad: Excessive Costs and Wasteful Spending

While Americans generally approve of the quality of their health care, its high cost is widely considered a serious problem. In 2001, the United States spent $4,887 per capita on medical care, or 13.9 percent of the gross domestic product (GDP), as compared to $2,792 in Canada (9.7 percent of GDP), $2,131 in Japan (8.0 percent), and $1,992 in the United Kingdom (7.6 percent).[12] Premiums for employer-sponsored health plans rose an astonishing 43 percent from 2000 to 2003.[13] Although Americans are generally pleased with the quality of care they receive, surveys show that they are not happy with its cost. In 2001, 71 percent reported feeling dissatisfied with the cost of health care—comparable to their level of dissatisfaction with domestic poverty, and far higher than their level of dissatisfaction with crime and the quality of education (see figure 2).[14]

However, spending a large share of GDP on medical care is not necessarily a cause for concern.[15] If the spending is "worth it"—if it improves the health of patients enough to justify the cost—then rising health spending should be of no greater concern than the increasing spending on, for example, information technology. The problem is that a lot of

FIGURE 2

HEALTH-CARE COSTS TOP LIST OF AMERICANS' DISSATISFACTION WITH STATE OF NATION

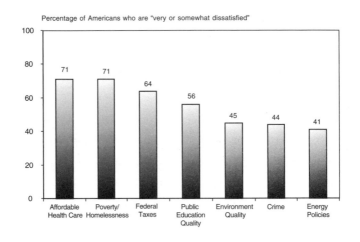

Percentage of Americans who are "very or somewhat dissatisfied"

SOURCE: "Survey Results on Cost of Health Care and Health Insurance," Market Strategies, Inc.: Livonia, Mich. (2004).

U.S. health-care spending provides few or no measurable health benefits for the individuals who receive the care. In many cases, diagnostic procedures and tests are overutilized, procedures are employed without tangible results, and expensive pharmaceuticals are unnecessarily prescribed.

Unfortunately, productive care and wasteful care are not so easy to tell apart. Even care that provides well-recognized benefits to the vast majority of patients often has minimal or no benefits for some, and perhaps many, people who receive it. Consider again the example of intensive cardiac treatment. No one would argue that the growth in intensive cardiac procedures was worthless. But as these procedures have diffused to greater numbers of people, the incremental benefits from further diffusion have declined.

Mark McClellan and colleagues, for example, compared treatment outcomes before and after the beginning of the high-tech revolution in cardiac procedures. They found that the greater likelihood of receiving intensive cardiac care among people living near high-tech hospitals led to only a modest (and possibly no) improvement in health.[16] Along these same lines, the study described in box 2 that found dramatic differences in the use of cardiac procedures across countries found much more modest differences in mortality and morbidity. Put another way, even if the difference in outcomes between a very parsimonious and a moderately generous country (in terms of procedure use) is substantial, the difference between a moderately generous country and a very generous one is not.

The same phenomenon exists for treatment of depression. According to Richard Frank and colleagues, approximately one-quarter of total spending on treatment of depression offers virtually no incremental benefit over nonintervention.[17]

As we elaborate below, the unintended consequences of a handful of public policies are responsible for much of this relatively wasteful health-care spending. The most important flaw in our current policy is the tax preference given to expenditures financed through insurance. Although there are a number of exceptions to this rule, the employer-paid portion of health-insurance costs is generally deductible to the employer and excludable from the calculation of both income and payroll taxes by the employee, but out-of-pocket expenditures must be made from after-tax income.

Economists have long noted two distortionary effects of this tax preference.[18] First, the exclusion from taxable income of compensation paid in the form of health insurance makes buying health care look less expensive to the worker than its actual cost to society. This observation holds true even for moderate-income workers with low income-tax rates, because their employer-provided health insurance is also not subject to payroll taxes.

Second, the exclusion of compensation paid in the form of health insurance makes buying health care through insurance instead of out-of-pocket look less expensive to the worker than it really is. This difference gives people the incentive to buy their medical care in ways that make them less conscious of its true cost.

The effect of low-deductible, low-copayment insurance on use of unproductive health-care services has been documented extensively, most notably by the RAND Corporation in the National Health Insurance Experiment.[19] The RAND study found that people enrolled in catastrophic health plans spent only about two-thirds as much on medical care as those in the full-coverage plan. Equally important, the study found that health outcomes of those in the catastrophic plans were, with few exceptions, no different from the outcomes for those in the full-coverage plan.

Various state laws have also contributed to the increasing volume of relatively unproductive expenditures. For example, mandated-benefits laws, which require health plans to cover particular types of persons, services, or providers (such as chiropractic services), increase health-insurance costs by at least 5 percent, and possibly as much as 15 percent.[20] Giving consumers the freedom to choose the benefits package they most prefer would save money and promote more responsible health-care spending decisions.

Similarly, "any-willing-provider" laws (which require health plans to accept bills from any doctor, hospital, or pharmacist who is willing to accept the plan's terms and conditions) increase costs by 1–2 percent by weakening the cost-containment effects of managed-care plans.[21] And the most costly states' malpractice systems increase expenditures on "defensive" medicine—treatment based on fear of litigation, which drives up costs but offers minimal health benefits—by approximately 3–7 percent among elderly Medicare beneficiaries with heart disease.[22] While each of these factors increases costs by just a few percentage points, their cumulative effect adds up to billions of dollars each year.

Research on the source of wasteful care contains a lesson closely related to that of research on the source of innovation: Just as public policy has the power to generate tremendous benefits when it takes appropriate account of incentives, so does it have the power to generate tremendous costs when it does not.

The Ugly: Uninsurance, the Managed-Care Backlash, and Medical Errors

Who lacks health insurance in America today—and why? Interestingly, it is difficult even to know how many Americans are without health insurance. Depending on the data source and definition of "uninsured," estimates range from 21 to 44 million (see box 3). Still, most agree that the uninsured are widely spread across the income spectrum. Approximately one-third are from households with incomes of at least $50,000 per year; one-third are less affluent but not poor enough to qualify for public assistance; and one-third are poor enough to qualify for publicly provided health insurance but do not sign up for coverage. Most of the new uninsured come from the most affluent group, many of whom are relatively healthy young adults.

Expanding rates of insurance among the better-off uninsured is an important step in fixing the health-care marketplace in America today. Well-functioning insurance markets require the participation of large numbers of individuals with widely varying degrees of health risks. When persons with low risks drop coverage, the entire insurance market is adversely affected, as their diminished presence in the insurance pool drives up the cost among those remaining. This outcome can cause the market to break down entirely, as it starts a vicious cycle in which each round of cost increases causes a further exodus of low-risk persons.

For the better-off uninsured, the lack of health insurance is less a failure of private markets that demands government intervention than an example of how public policies have caused the problems we now face. By increasing the cost to workers of employer-provided health insurance, the federal and state tax and regulatory policies discussed above have had social consequences far beyond their direct financial implications. From 2000 to 2003, the average monthly worker contribution for standard family insurance coverage increased by $63, from $138 per month to $201 per month.[23] The inevitable result has been an increase in uninsurance. Ironically, this decline in coverage rates has produced additional calls for more extensive regulation.

Providing health insurance to the 14 million people who are already eligible for public programs but do not accept it is a different challenge. Approximately half of this group was offered but declined private coverage.[24] Furthermore, future expansions of public insurance programs like Medicaid are likely to suffer more than past expansions from this "takeup" problem. Takeup was close to complete in the 1980s, before the major Medicaid expansions, but it has fallen considerably over time as more people have become eligible.[25] The causes of the low rate of takeup of public programs in general, and the Medicaid program in particular, are an ongoing puzzle for researchers. A recent survey of the literature reports that several factors contribute to the takeup problem, including the inferiority of program benefits, inconvenience, cultural attitudes and stigma, and poor information.[26]

Tax and regulatory policies have contributed to a second problem in health-care markets: the so-called "managed-care backlash." In 2003, Americans rated managed-care and health-insurance companies more unfavorably than every other industry (see figure 3 on

Box 3

WHO ARE THE UNINSURED?

Estimates of how many Americans are without health insurance vary widely. Current Population Survey (CPS) data show that 44 million people were uninsured at some point during 1998.[27] Many fewer people were without insurance for the entire year. According to the Congressional Budget Office's analysis of data from the Census Bureau's Survey of Income and Program Participation, 21.1 million Americans were uninsured for the entire year of 1998; estimates based on the Medical Expenditure Panel Survey indicate 31.1 million uninsured people that same year.[28]

The uninsured can be divided into three groups of approximately equal size. One-third, about 14 million persons in 2001, are low-income and eligible for government health-insurance programs, such as Medicaid and the State Children's Health Insurance Program (SCHIP), but do not sign up for coverage.[29] During the 1970s and '80s, the federal and state governments initiated outreach programs to encourage greater participation. In spite of this, the problem of eligible individuals failing to enroll continues to plague these programs.

The approximate one-third of the uninsured whose incomes are at least $50,000 is the only income group in which uninsurance is growing: from 1998 to 2001, rates of uninsurance fell among all income groups below $50,000.[30] One likely reason for the decline in insurance coverage among the more affluent is the rapid increase in health-insurance premiums due to escalating health costs. State mandated-benefits and any-willing-provider laws raise insurance costs, which contribute to

(continued on next page)

(Box 3, continued)

uninsurance, without providing a commensurate increase in value.

Finally, approximately one-third of uninsured Americans are low-income but not currently eligible for government programs. Many of these individuals are without insurance for a relatively short period of time. The Congressional Budget Office found that only 18 percent of uninsured individuals with family incomes of less than 200 percent of the poverty line were uninsured for more than two years; 42 percent of uninsured individuals with family incomes of less than 200 percent of the poverty line were uninsured for less than four months.[31]

---

page 22).[32] Fully 52 percent of people polled said that the government needed to protect consumers from being treated unfairly and not getting the care they should from managed-care plans.[33]

Managed care was, at least in part, the solution markets offered to the problem of relatively unproductive health-care expenditures induced by policy. Health-care experts widely agree that managed care played a central role in slowing medical expenditure growth during the 1990s. In response to the incentives provided by managed care, providers curtailed the growth in spending on enrollees. In addition, competition from managed-care plans forced conventional private insurers and public insurance programs to reduce the growth in spending.[34] But managed care failed to change

FIGURE 3

HEALTH CARE IS THE MOST NEGATIVELY
PERCEIVED BUSINESS SECTOR

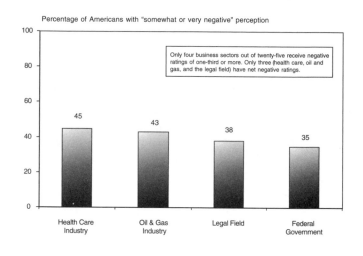

Percentage of Americans with "somewhat or very negative" perception

> Only four business sectors out of twenty-five receive negative ratings of one-third or more. Only three (health care, oil and gas, and the legal field) have net negative ratings.

SOURCE: "Survey Results on Cost of Health Care and Health Insurance," Market Strategies Inc.

the incentives that underlay individual patients' demands for health-care services and, as a result, enrollees continued to demand high levels of service. When high demand met curtailed supply, the backlash was the result.

The gap between patients' expectations and the supply of care is another unintended consequence of U.S. tax policy. To date, managed care has relied heavily on administrative approaches, such as gatekeepers, rather than cost-conscious consumers to control resource use. In doing so, it has deprived patients of decision-making authority. The tax preference for insurance creates powerful incentives for the health-care system to favor gatekeepers over deductibles and copayments. The cost of gatekeepers is financed out of insurance premiums that are paid with before-tax dollars. In contrast, deductibles and copayments, tools for making consumers cost conscious, are paid with after-tax dollars. For this reason, gatekeepers start with a built-in advantage.

Finally, poorly designed policy has contributed to the problem of medical errors. Medical errors are the leading cause of accidental death in the United States, producing at least 44,000 and perhaps as many as 98,000 deaths in 1997.[35] Medication errors alone account for approximately 7,000 deaths per year, exceeding the number due to workplace injuries. One study found that nearly 1 percent of hospital admissions in New York State in 1984 involved an injury due to negligent care; the proportion of serious injuries due to negligence was even higher.[36] More recent research has found similar rates of iatrogenic injury in Utah and Colorado in 1992.[37]

A key obstacle to reducing the number of medical errors is the ability of plaintiffs in medical malpractice lawsuits to discover data collected as part of quality-improvement initiatives. States provide varying levels of statutory protection to analyses of medical errors within individual health-care organizations through "peer-review protection" laws, but analyses that involve information-sharing across organizations are largely unprotected. By allowing plaintiffs to use quality-improvement initiatives against malpractice defendants, current law gives doctors, hospitals, and insurers a disincentive to collect information on medical errors. But this is exactly the wrong signal to send; public policy should encourage investment to reduce medical errors, not discourage it.

Although the *extent* to which poorly designed public policies are responsible for uninsurance, political backlash, and harm from medical errors is an open topic for debate, the *fact* that they have played a major role in causing these problems is not. According to the Congressional Budget Office, each increase of one percentage point in the price of health insurance leads to approximately 300,000 more uninsured.[38] Public policies that drive up insurance costs, inhibit competition, and give providers a distorted signal about the care people need have significant, adverse effects on a large number of lives.

2

Five Policy Reforms to Make Markets Work

Although America's health-care system is strong in many respects, poorly designed public policies have created significant problems as well: relatively unproductive care; a growing number of people without health insurance; an increase in bureaucratic controls with a corresponding loss of personal and medical authority; and an excessive number of medical errors. Many interpret these problems as evidence that markets are the wrong way to deliver health care. The problem, though, is not that market forces cannot work in health care. Rather, public policies have prevented health-care markets from functioning properly.

The tax preference for employer health insurance has created a health-care system in which doctors and patients bear few of the resource costs of their decisions. In this perverse world, true insurance, in the form of coverage for catastrophic health events, is the exception; prepaid health care, in the form of coverage with low deductibles and copayments, is the rule.

The pervasiveness of prepaid health care instead of true insurance, in turn, encourages the consumption of relatively unproductive care. Inefficient regulation prevents people from purchasing the type of insurance that they want. In addition, the malpractice system has both encouraged wasteful expenditures and discouraged investment in addressing the problem of medical errors.

When combined with technological improvements, these policies inevitably lead to rising costs. In response, the system has sought to limit cost growth through the use of administrative controls such as gatekeepers, rather than cost-conscious consumers. The overuse of gatekeepers has had numerous and potentially profound adverse effects: the direct cost of the extra gatekeepers; the loss of consumer decision-making authority; and the damage to the prospects of developing effective public policies caused by the public perception that markets do not work in health care.

Despite the shortcomings of current policy, the infrastructure for improving the functioning of markets is nonetheless in place. Flexible spending accounts and health-reimbursement accounts provided by employers, medical savings accounts, and recently enacted health savings accounts allow consumers to incorporate more of the true treatment costs in their decisions.

Five policy changes would further promote more efficient purchasing of medical care, stimulate a vigorous, competitive market for insurance, expand coverage of the currently uninsured, and reduce medical errors:

1. Change the tax law to reduce the preference for medical-care purchases through employer-based health insurance.

2. Reform regulation of markets for health insurance.

3. Expand provision of health information.

4. Control anticompetitive behavior by providers and insurers.

5. Reform the malpractice system.

Finally, we propose that a sixth potential reform be studied further: revocation or limitation of the current tax preference for nonprofits.

Reform Taxation of Health-Care Expenses

Preferential treatment of employer-paid health-insurance costs by public policy began with a seemingly innocuous provision of the Stabilization Act of 1942, which limited the wage increases that employers could grant but permitted employer-paid health insurance to be provided as a fringe benefit exempt from wage controls. The preference was extended to the tax code shortly thereafter. Under a 1943 administrative tax-court ruling and 1954 changes to the

Internal Revenue Code, employer contributions to employee health-insurance costs became deductible to the employer and nontaxable to the employee.[1]

This tax preference has never been absolute, however. Extraordinary medical expenses paid out of pocket have long been deductible to varying degrees. Under the Revenue Act of 1942, medical expenses in excess of 5 percent of a taxpayer's adjusted gross income, up to $2,500, qualified as an itemized deduction.[2] The floor for the medical-expense deduction was lowered to 3 percent (and the ceiling was raised) in 1954; the floor was raised back to 5 percent in 1982 and raised again to its current 7.5 percent level in 1986.[3]

The tax preference has created a strong financial incentive for individuals to purchase medical care through employer-provided insurance. Neither employer nor employee pays income or payroll taxes on the employer's contribution to an employee's insurance plan. By contrast, a worker who purchases health insurance on his own must finance the purchase with after-tax income—that is, income that remains after income and payroll taxes have been deducted. A typical middle-income worker faces a marginal federal income-tax rate of 15 percent and a payroll-tax rate on wages of 7.65 percent. An employer must also pay a payroll tax of 7.65 percent on wages, raising the total marginal tax rate on wage income to approximately 30 percent.

By purchasing health insurance through the employer, these taxes are avoided, and, together, the employer and employee save almost one-third of the cost of a health-care plan compared to having the employee purchase medical care or health insurance on his own. At least in part due to the tax preference, 1/4 million out of 198 million persons who are covered by private health insurance are enrolled in employer-sponsored plans.[4]

Similarly, the tax preference has also created large incentives to purchase employer-provided insurance with low deductibles and copayment rates, even though such plans cost considerably more than catastrophic health insurance. Several studies conclude that revoking the tax preference for employer-provided insurance would lead the effective coinsurance rate to double.[5] For employers, this change would translate into average premiums for group health insurance that were 45 percent lower.[6]

These estimates, though at least a decade old, are consistent with current evidence. According to unpublished data for 2003 from Anthem, a large health insurer, the average annual deductible among plans purchased through large firms (500 or more employees), and hence excluded from taxation, was $250; the average deductible among plans purchased directly by individuals, most of which were purchased with after-tax income, was $1,250, or five times greater.[7]

Health plans with low deductibles and coinsurance rates create a "moral hazard" that leads patients and their physicians to use too many services that do little to improve measurable health outcomes. According to the RAND Corporation's National Health Insurance Experiment, an increase in a health plan's annual deductible from $200 to $500 reduces the total amount an individual spends on health care through both insurance and out-of-pocket payments by nearly 5 percent.[8]

Similarly, an increase in a plan's coinsurance rate from 25 to 35 percent reduces the total amount an individual spends on health-care services by approximately 8 percent.[9] Although these percentages might seem small, when aggregated over the entire population with private health insurance, the impact is large. Each percentage-point increase in health-care spending among this group equals $7 billion a year. And, these changes occur without any appreciable impact on most individuals' measurable health outcomes.[10]

Thus, the tax preference for buying medical care through employer-sponsored insurance is largely responsible for creating today's health-insurance market, in which third parties pay five out of every six dollars spent on medical-care services, and individual consumers and health-care providers exhibit little cost consciousness. Elected officials, however, have been unwilling to eliminate the tax exclusion for employer-provided insurance, presumably because it would significantly raise taxes on a broad class of taxpayers.

To make this point clear, consider a household facing a combined marginal income- and payroll-tax rate of 30 percent. Suppose that the household's employer makes a $6,600 annual contribution to the household's health-insurance plan.[11] Repealing the tax exclusion would increase this household's taxes by approximately $2,000. Higher-income households with employer-sponsored insurance would have their taxes raised by more, and lower-income households would have their taxes raised by less. But all 175 million persons who are covered by employer-sponsored insurance would have taxes on their wage compensation increased.

Only President Reagan expressed a willingness to consider repealing the health-insurance tax exclusion. In 1983, he proposed to cap the amount of employer-provided insurance that could be excluded from taxation. His proposal was soundly rejected in Congress. A similar proposal was considered and rejected during the 1985 tax-reform debate. Since then, no president has proposed to modify the exclusion for employer-provided health insurance. Today, when Americans are registering unprecedented concerns about the high cost of health care, a policy that would significantly raise this cost would likely face insurmountable legislative hurdles.

Since the late 1970s, the federal government has taken an alternative, incremental approach to removing the tax bias that favors health insurance over out-of-pocket payments. The approach has been to exclude from taxation out-of-pocket payments under certain conditions.

First, changes in 1978 to section 125 of the Internal Revenue Code allowed expenditures made through an employer's "cafeteria" plan to be deductible to the employer but nontaxable to the employee. A cafeteria plan is a benefits plan that allows employees to allocate a portion of their compensation to nontaxable fringe benefits instead of taxable wages. Currently, once the amount of the cafeteria-plan contribution has been designated, the employee is not allowed to change it or drop the plan during the year unless he or she experiences a change of family status. By law, the employee forfeits any unspent funds in the account at the end of the year.[12]

This result has the unfortunate effect of creating incentives for individuals who have unspent funds near year's end to consume more health-care services simply to avoid forfeiting the funds. Prior to Treasury Department regulations issued in 1984, there was no such "use-it-or-lose-it" provision implied by section 125, making the cafeteria-plan exception even more generous to employees.[13]

Second, under Treasury regulations issued in 2002, sections 105 and 106 of the Internal Revenue Code allow "health-reimbursement arrangements," also known as "health-reimbursement accounts" or "personal-care accounts," to reimburse employees for medical expenses with before-tax dollars, without the use-it-or-lose-it provision of section 125 cafeteria plans.[14]

Third, under the Medicare Prescription Drug, Improvement, and Modernization Act of 2003, employers and individuals with qualifying health-insurance plans can make tax-free contributions to health savings accounts. Funds from these accounts can be used to pay for medical expenses in the present or the future. However, the fact that qualifying plans must have very high deductibles has limited the takeup of these accounts.

We propose to build on this approach by making three simple changes in tax policy to promote more efficient insurance policy design, to offer incentives for consumers to be better shoppers, and to enhance tax fairness. These changes are the allowance of full deductibility of health-care expenses, expanded health savings accounts, and tax credits for low-income individuals.

Full Deductibility of Health-Care Expenses. All Americans should be entitled to deduct expenditures on health insurance and out-of-pocket health-care expenses as long as they purchase insurance that covers at least catastrophic expenditures. That is, individuals already covered by employer-sponsored insurance may deduct out-of-pocket expenses and their employee contributions. Self-employed individuals with insurance may deduct out-of-pocket expenses. Individuals currently without coverage may deduct insurance premiums and out-of-pocket expenses if they choose to purchase an insurance plan. (In all cases, the deduction is "above the line"—available even to taxpayers not itemizing income-tax deductions.)[15]

Allowing direct individual payments for health care to be tax deductible promotes insurance that provides financial protection from catastrophic illness or injury, and yet creates significant incentives for individuals to be cost conscious in their decisions about health care. We call such insurance "true" insurance. The policy does so by reducing the tax bias against out-of-pocket health expenditures.

Under the current tax treatment, any medical care purchased through employer-sponsored insurance is paid for with pretax dollars, while care purchased out of pocket is paid for with after-tax dollars. Recall from our previous example that, even for a middle-income family, the differential is substantial, amounting to approximately 30 percent when both federal income and payroll taxes are considered. Once the tax bias is reduced, individuals will find it in their financial interest to purchase health plans with lower premiums and higher copayments (see box 4), a shift that will give them incentives to make careful choices about their health-care spending, as well as the opportunity to save money.

In addition, allowing direct health-care expenses to be tax deductible will significantly reduce the growth in health costs, as greater cost consciousness leads to less spending. Below, we show that for any plausible set of parameter values, this curtailment of spending will more than offset any increase in out-of-pocket spending that occurs because tax deductibility lowers the cost of health-care spending compared to other goods.

Our proposal for full deductibility has several other beneficial effects. Deductibility mitigates the bias against individual insurance because both employer-sponsored and individual insurance can be acquired with pre–income tax dollars. However, because the tax change allows the deduction of the cost of individual insurance from the income-tax base but not from the payroll-tax base, the proposed policy retains a significant tax incentive for the purchase of employer-sponsored insurance. Expenditures on insurance purchased through an employer would, as under current law, still be excludable from both the income- and payroll-tax bases.

Because the tax change allows the deductibility of out-of-pocket health-care expenses only with the purchase of insurance, the proposed policy also creates a significant tax incentive for the currently uninsured to purchase insurance.

Under current law, a typical uninsured person receives no tax benefit from purchasing coverage. Under our proposal, an individual who purchased a $2,000 health plan and also paid $1,000 in out-of-pocket expenses would not only be able to deduct the cost of out-of-pocket expenses, but also his health-insurance premiums. Indeed, for a person in the 15 percent tax bracket, the tax deduction is worth $450—23 percent of the cost of insurance.

The tax change also enhances the fairness of the federal income-tax system. Under current law, individuals whose employers decline to offer them insurance are penalized because they must purchase it with after-tax income. Tax deductibility would promote simplicity by replacing the myriad of currently available special health-care deductions discussed above with a single deduction equally applicable to all individuals. Finally, as we show below, deductibility would also increase the progressivity of the tax system. Although marginal tax rates are higher for higher-income people, the fact that lower-income people have higher (currently taxable) out-of-pocket spending more than compensates for this effect.

Modified Health Savings Accounts. The tax code can also be changed to make it easier for individuals and families to save for expenses not covered by higher-deductible insurance. Medical savings accounts (MSAs) and recently enacted health savings accounts (HSAs) currently permit tax-free contributions for individuals purchasing high-deductible health-insurance plans. We propose making all individuals eligible

Box 4

How Full Deductibility Promotes Cost-Conscious Insurance

Consider a family that expects to spend $3,600 on health care in the coming year and is concerned that it could end up spending a lot more. Suppose the family's employer offers a choice between a health plan with a high annual premium ($5,400) that requires no deductible and a plan with a lower annual premium ($3,000) that has a deductible of $1,800. For simplicity, assume that the coinsurance rate for expenses above the deductible is zero. If the family chooses the latter plan, the employer will increase the family's salary income by the amount of the premium savings, less the additional payroll taxes the employer is required to withhold (7.65 percent).

Under current tax law, the family will choose the zero-deductible plan. If the family chooses the $1,800-deductible plan, it will receive $2,216 from the employer (the premium savings of $2,400, less the employer's share of payroll taxes of $184). But because the family is required to pay an additional $502 in income and payroll taxes (= $2,216 x 15 percent federal income tax plus 7.65 percent payroll tax), it receives only $1,714. This total is $86 less than the expected increase in the family's out-of-pocket expenditures under the $1,800-deductible plan.

If out-of-pocket expenses were tax deductible, however, the family would choose the $1,800-deductible plan. The family would realize a tax savings of $270 (= $1,800 x 15 percent federal income tax) from its higher out-of-pocket health-care spending under the

(continued on next page)

(BOX 4, *continued*)

$1,800-deductible plan. Thus, its net tax burden would rise by only $232 (= $502 − $270) instead of $502. The family's after-tax income would, therefore, rise by $1,984 (= $2,216 − $232). This increase is $184 more than the expected increase in the family's out-of-pocket expenditures under the $1,800-deductible plan.

for health savings accounts, conditional on the purchase of insurance that covers at least catastrophic expenditures. As with current HSAs, balances may be spent on the health care of a relative, and balances not spent on health care could be carried forward tax-free. Funds withdrawn for purposes other than health care would be subject to income tax. Recipients of health-care tax credits (described below) could deposit funds in a health savings account, if they wished.

We propose three significant changes to HSAs. First, under current law, an employer-sponsored family health-insurance plan must have a deductible of at least $2,000 to qualify its purchaser for the HSA ($1,000 for an individual plan). We should eliminate the minimum deductible requirement.

Second, the amount a household can deposit in an HSA is currently limited to the amount of the health-insurance plan deductible, up to a maximum of $5,150 ($2,600 for an individual plan). We propose setting a $2,000 limit ($1,000 for individuals) on the amount that can be deposited in an HSA, independent of the plan deductible.

Third, under current law, funds from an HSA cannot be used to purchase insurance. Under our proposal, funds from an HSA can be used for any qualified health-care expense.

The purpose of these proposed changes is to make the HSA law less prescriptive and, thereby, encourage greater use of HSAs. We are concerned that the high-deductible requirement under current law may serve as an important barrier to widespread use of HSAs. Under our proposal, individuals would be free to choose the deductible level, make tradeoffs between the deductible and coinsurance amounts, and purchase insurance on their own rather than through an employer, all without tax penalty. Consistent with our policy of full deductibility, we believe that public policy should, whenever possible, allow individual preferences rather than government mandates to determine people's health-insurance arrangements.

Tax Credits for Low-Income Individuals. A third policy we support is designed to improve the health-care "safety net" for very-low-income households. While our proposal to make out-of-pocket medical expenses tax-deductible offers important benefits for many low- and middle-income working families, it does not help families that pay little or no income tax.

To address this inequity, we should offer low-income households financial assistance to purchase health-care services. Specifically, we propose a refundable tax credit that would subsidize 25 percent of household health-care expenses up to a maximum credit of $500 for an individual or $1,000 for a family. Health-care expenses would include both payments for insurance and out-of-pocket expenses. Thus, the refundable credit would be available to buy insurance through an employer, on one's own, or to pay for out-of-pocket expenses (conditional on having insurance).

The full subsidy should be available to insured households with income below the poverty level. The subsidy would be gradually phased out for households with incomes between 100 and 300 percent of the poverty level. Tax subsidies of this magnitude would cover a substantial portion of the cost of an individual catastrophic insurance policy (see box 5). Low-income households could not claim both the tax deduction for direct medical expenses and the tax credit, but instead would be required to choose between the two.

Our tax-reform policies will encourage people to substitute true insurance for their current prepaid health-care arrangements. These policies enhance the incentives for people to use their own out-of-pocket payments or savings rather than third parties to finance ordinary health expenses. This substitution will lead health costs and, in turn, rates of uninsurance to decline. At the same time, these policies enhance the incentives for uninsured people to purchase insurance, make the tax system fairer, and offer a direct benefit to low- and middle-income people to help them meet rising health costs. Collectively, by reducing the current tax bias against low-cost catastrophic insurance, these policies will help develop a more robust market for such insurance. Box 6 summarizes the tax benefits for the purchase of health insurance in our proposals.

Box 5

True Insurance Is Affordable

The effect of our proposed tax reforms on health-insurance purchases depends in part on what type of insurance is available for consumers to buy. Some reports have placed the "mid-range" cost of family health insurance at about $7,000 per year, which is large relative to the tax subsidies we propose.[16] But this estimate reflects the average, not the best offer available for the typical uninsured family. More important, the high cost of such plans reflects the tax code's bias toward inefficient, first-dollar health insurance—a bias that would be reduced as a result of our reforms.

Preferred provider organization (PPO) family policies with premiums significantly lower than $7,000 are almost always available. These plans typically cover all major types of medical services and treatment, have per-person deductibles of $1,000 ($2,000 or $3,000 for a family) while also covering preventative and emergency care, and support a range of provider choices. A 2002 survey by the Council of Economic Advisers found that the median annual premium for a plan of this type was $2,683 for a family of four, $1,518 for a mother and child, and $772 for a young male.[17] PPO-type plans offer individuals choice, assistance with access to the full range of modern health-care treatments, and insurance protection against large, unanticipated expenses caused by severe illness or needed surgery. Patients who prefer lower copayments could choose an HMO-style plan that uses more restrictive networks and tighter control of care to keep premiums low.

(*continued on next page*)

(Box 5, *continued*)

But is this "affordable" for the typical uninsured person? A recent study by Kate Bundorf and Mark Pauly combines data on premiums for policies offered in the individual insurance market with data on uninsured people's incomes to investigate this question. Depending on the definition of "affordable," they find that health insurance was affordable to between one-quarter and three-quarters of the uninsured in 2000.[18]

Reform Regulation of Markets for Health Insurance

Under the 1944 McCarran-Ferguson Act, states have primary responsibility for regulating health-insurance markets. Each of the fifty states specifies the rules by which its insurance market operates, including the financial requirements insurers must meet in order to sell policies in the state, the particular services that a health-insurance plan must cover, the prices insurers can charge, the individuals or groups that must be offered coverage, and the method by which insurance companies must conduct their business operations.

For example, New York State requires insurance companies to offer coverage at the same price to all persons within a given age and gender group regardless of health status; most other states allow insurers to consider an individual's health status in setting premiums in the individual market.

Box 6

**TAX BENEFITS FOR THE PURCHASE OF HEALTH INSURANCE:
CURRENT LAW AND PROPOSAL**

	Current Law	**Proposed Law**
Individuals with Employer-Provided Insurance		
	Employer-paid premiums excluded from income and payroll taxes; out-of-pocket expenses and employee premium payments generally not deductible.	Employer-paid premiums continue to be excluded from both income and payroll taxation; out-of-pocket expenses and employee premium payments would be deductible from income taxes, but not payroll taxes.
	Individuals with high-deductible insurance plans can make tax-free contributions to limited federal health-care accounts, such as MSAs, and cafeteria plans. Contributions to health savings accounts, for example, can be made up to the amount of the plan's annual deductible, but not more than $2,600 for individuals ($5,150 for families).	Tax-free contributions to health savings accounts of $2,000 ($1,000 for individuals) could be made regardless of the health plan's deductible level.
		Health-care tax credit covering 25 percent of insurance and out-of-pocket expenses up to $1,000 for families in poverty covered by insurance ($500 for individuals in poverty).

(*continued on next page*)

(Box 6, *continued*)

	Current Law	Proposed Law
Individuals without Employer-Provided Insurance		
Self-employed	Premiums deductible for purposes of income but not payroll taxes; out-of-pocket expenses generally not deductible. Deductibility of health savings accounts as above.	Premiums continue to be deductible from income but not payroll taxes; out-of-pocket expenses deductible if person is covered by insurance. Tax-free contributions to health savings accounts of $2,000 ($1,000 for individuals) could be made regardless of the health plan's deductible level. Health-care tax credit covering 25 percent of health-care insurance and out-of-pocket expenses up to $1,000 for families in poverty covered by insurance ($500 for individuals in poverty).
All others	Neither premiums nor out-of-pocket expenses are generally deductible. Medical savings accounts are not allowed. Deductibility of health savings accounts as above.	

Many states also require that specific benefits and providers be covered by all health-insurance plans.

In 1965, there were less than a dozen such mandates in laws throughout the fifty states and the District of

Columbia; by 2003, the number had risen to over 1,800.[19] For example, California requires insurance plans to cover both contraceptives and in-vitro fertilization; Virginia requires coverage of contraceptives but not in-vitro fertilization; and Florida, Indiana, and Pennsylvania require coverage of neither service.[20]

In addition, some states have adopted laws, termed "any-willing-provider" laws, that require health plans to reimburse expenses for care provided by any doctor, hospital, or pharmacist who is willing to accept the plans' terms and conditions. Such laws stifle health plans' ability to require providers to compete with one another to improve quality and contain costs.

States' mandated-benefits and regulatory actions drive up the cost of insurance significantly. Mandates have raised the cost of a typical insurance plan by at least 5 percent, to possibly as much as 15 percent.[21] Any-willing-provider laws drive up health-care costs by as much as 1.8 percent.[22] In turn, the rising costs imposed by benefits mandates and regulation have reduced the number of persons with health insurance. Although there is considerable uncertainty about the precise magnitude of the reduction, one study estimates about 25 percent of the people who are without health insurance are uninsured because of the cost of state mandates alone.[23]

The highly prescriptive state regulation of insurance allowed under the McCarran-Ferguson Act, however, has been partially preempted by the Employee Retirement and Income Security Act (ERISA) of 1974. Under ERISA, health-care plans offered by firms that self-insure are exempt from many of these costly state regulations. Instead, ERISA plans are subject to much less prescriptive regulation by the federal government. For example, there are no regulations controlling the premiums that employers can charge as long as they are the same for all employees, and there is significantly less regulation of benefits.

Heavy state regulation, with an exception for firms that self-insure, has been particularly damaging to the small-group market and the market for individual insurance. State regulation has caused many large employers to self-insure and, thereby, opt out of the state-regulated insurance market. In 2001, 47 percent of all employees in employer-sponsored plans were in plans subject to federal, as opposed to state, regulation. Thus, the cost burden of state mandates and regulations has been increasingly borne by persons who purchase health insurance on their own and employees of small firms that purchase state-regulated insurance.

If present trends continue, the burden of state mandates and regulations will fall on an increasingly narrower class of persons. Large employers will continue to opt for federal instead of state regulation. In addition, the Small Business Health Fairness Act recently passed by the House of Representatives would permit small firms to join together to offer insurance plans that are exempt from state regulation.[24] These "Association Health Plans" would be subject to federal regulations similar to those that govern self-funded employers.

We propose two sets of reforms to regulation of markets for health insurance: First, allow insurers to offer plans on a nationwide basis, free from costly state benefit mandates and regulation; and second, subsidize the costs of caring for persistently high-cost, chronically ill patients.

Foster Nationwide, Portable Health Insurance. The key objective of insurance reform is to improve the availability and portability of low-cost health insurance. We propose that insurance companies that meet certain federal standards be permitted to offer plans on a nationwide basis free from costly state mandates, rules, and regulations. Hence, insurance would become available to individuals and small groups on the same terms and conditions as those currently offered to employees of many large corporations under ERISA.

The federally certified health-insurance products would be required to meet all federal regulations that currently govern the provision of health insurance for large employers under ERISA; there would be no rollback of existing federal protections. Insurance companies that offer federally certified products would be required to meet financial structure and solvency requirements. In addition, states could continue to supervise day-to-day market conduct. Finally, insurance companies that offer federally certified products would no longer be exempt from federal antitrust statutes under the McCarran-Ferguson Act.

There are several benefits to creating a federally certified market for health insurance. Most important, this change will foster a more competitive, efficient market for nongroup health insurance that will offer individuals a greater variety of lower-cost insurance alternatives. As noted above, freedom from state-imposed mandate and provider requirements alone has been estimated to reduce the cost of insurance by 5–15 percent. The lower cost is expected to induce more persons to buy insurance and, thereby, increase the size of risk pools.

The reform will also create several ancillary benefits. First, it will increase the portability of health insurance. Families who currently purchase insurance in the individual or small-group market in one state often must drop that coverage and find new insurance when moving to another state. At a minimum, this exposes the family to unnecessary financial risks. With nationwide competitively priced insurance plans available, the potential loss of insurance will no longer be a barrier to geographical relocation.

Second, the policy change will create a more level playing field between families who must obtain insurance in the nongroup market and those who work for large employers whose plans are exempt from costly state regulations. And the reduction in costs will lead to a decline in the uninsured.

One objection to this proposal is that it represents a federal intrusion to an area that has been historically reserved to the states. Allowing health plans to receive federal certification may eventually lead to even more regulation than occurs under state law. Congress, by enacting a single policy change, is capable of imposing broad regulations across the entire U.S. health-care market. If the individual states retained jurisdiction, separate actions by fifty state legislatures would be required to achieve the same regulatory outcome. Although this concern is not without foundation, the obvious benefits to consumers of a federal market outweigh the potential costs.

First, the regulation of private health insurance is by no means the exclusive province of the states. As discussed above, since the enactment of ERISA in the mid-1970s, the federal government has had a significant presence in health-insurance markets. About one-half of all privately insured individuals are in plans that are subject to federal, not state, regulation.

Second, although the past is no guarantee of the future, there are practical reasons to believe that an appropriately structured federal market would be regulated more efficiently than state markets. The federally regulated market would continue to be dominated by self-funded health-insurance plans offered primarily by large businesses. As they have in the past, these employers would present a strong barrier to benefit mandates and other inefficient regulations. Importantly, the proposal seeks to extend to all individuals the political protection provided by well-organized large employers to their workers. Indeed, the exit of large employers from state-regulated insurance markets since the passage of ERISA in the mid-1970s, and the resulting absence of this protection, has been one reason for the extraordinary rise in state benefit-mandates.

Our reform builds on the George W. Bush administration's proposal to allow individuals and small groups to shop across state lines for insurance.[25] Although allowing interstate shopping can help instigate a national market in insurance, it has two potential drawbacks, to the extent that it essentially assigns all regulatory responsibility to the insurer's state. This could be problematic if it encourages states to choose regulatory regimes that externalize costs onto insureds who live elsewhere. In addition, assigning all responsibility to the insurer's state will be vigorously resisted by some state insurance regulators and consumer groups. This resistance will inevitably result in lawsuits in state courts and/or congressional action, and the consequent uncertainty will inhibit firms from participating in the new market. For these reasons, some formal, compromise apportionment of regulatory responsibility among the insurer's state, the insured's state, and the federal government is necessary; the apportionment we suggest is only one among many feasible policy options.

Subsidize Insurance for the Chronically Ill. One of health policy's most vexing problems is providing affordable health insurance for chronically ill persons who have predictably high medical expenses year after year and lack sufficient resources to finance them. Competitive markets for insurance, which provide good protection for *unforeseen* major medical expenses, do not work well for persistently high-cost patients.

States have responded to the problem of the chronically ill in two ways, both of them unsatisfactory. High-risk pools, in theory, allow individuals who have been denied coverage or charged a high premium due to their health status to obtain subsidized insurance. In 1999, although twenty-eight states operated high-risk pools, they covered a total of only 105,000 individuals.[26] The authors of this study concluded that the small size of pool enrollment is due to several factors, including high costs, limited benefits, limited outreach to prospective members, and, in some cases, explicitly capped enrollment.[27]

State insurance premium risk-bands and underwriting restrictions limit the range of premiums and the characteristics on which they can be based. However, a study of regulation of the small-group insurance market found that stringent regulations of this form decreased the rate of coverage among workers and increased premiums for small employers, and that most of the increase was passed on to workers through higher employee contributions.[28]

Only a subset of the people who have high health-care costs in any given year will have difficulty obtaining coverage: those who are nonelderly and nondisabled (the elderly and disabled are eligible for Medicare), with high costs that are predictable and persistent. A person who suffers a catastrophic health event that is unpredictable and short-lived would be just as able to purchase insurance afterward as a person who did not suffer the event, because the event would (by definition) have a minimal effect on future health expenses. The terminally ill, although high-cost, are disproportionately elderly and disabled, and so are already provided insurance by Medicare.

We propose making persons suffering from chronic illness eligible for a public subsidy to purchase insurance in the nationwide private insurance market. A public-private partnership between the federal government and insurance companies would administer the subsidy. In order to be eligible for it, chronically ill persons would be required to have been covered by insurance in the past and have insufficient resources to pay for their own coverage.

The subsidy would provide partial coverage to an eligible person free of charge that would begin to cover health-care expenses when they exceeded a specified multiple of that person's area-average expenses. The partial insurance could only be used with a basic wrap-around policy purchased from an insurer in the federal market. The subsidy could be implemented through a uniform federal program, or through block grants to the states.

This subsidy would preserve coverage for the chronically ill at a lower cost than its alternatives, and without the unintended consequences and market distortions created by them. One alternative, for example, seeks to socialize the costs of all high-cost patients. Such socialization helps the chronically ill, but it also subsidizes the catastrophically ill—those with unexpectedly high costs that will not persist, such as individuals injured in auto accidents. Private insurance markets, however, work well at financing the care of the catastrophically ill; adverse selection arises only when a patient's (high) expenditures are predictable in advance.

The extra cost of this alternative could be substantial. According to a 2003 study based on the Medical Expenditures Panel Survey, a large fraction of individuals who have high costs in one year do not have them in subsequent years.[29] The top 1 percent of users of health-care service in 1996 accounted for 27.9 percent of all health-care expenditures, the top 5 percent for 56.0 percent, and the top 10 percent for 69.8 percent.[30] However, only 13.7 percent of the top 1 percent of 1996 spenders were in the top 1 percent of 1997 spenders; approximately half of the top 1 percent of 1996 spenders remained in the top 10 percent.

Expand Provision of Health Information

If health-care markets are to work effectively and consumers are to make wise choices about their care, they need more access to better information about quality and cost. We focus on two approaches to improving the provision of health information: report cards and clinical practice guidelines.

Report cards collect and disseminate data on the quality of doctors, hospitals, nursing homes, and health plans (see box 7). Clinical practice guidelines specify the right kind of treatment for a specific illness, set of symptoms, or type of patient. Both the public and private sectors have developed extensive sets of report cards and clinical practice guidelines. Yet surveys of health-services research provide at best equivocal evidence of the effectiveness of these vehicles for improving consumer information.[31]

We propose two initiatives to enhance the effectiveness of report cards and clinical practice guidelines. First, we propose supporting a privately produced portfolio of different types of report cards with public funds and publicly collected data. As with many grants through the U.S. Department of Health and Human Services (HHS) and the National Institutes of Health (NIH), these grants could be accompanied by permission to use health-insurance claims and mortality data from individual states or the Medicare and Medicaid programs. Indeed, HHS and NIH already provide such confidential data to researchers for this and similar purposes. In particular, we would emphasize research that seeks to measure the effects on patient decision

Box 7

CALIFORNIA'S HEALTHSCOPE

One model for a new generation of report cards is provided by HealthScope, an independent report card produced by the Pacific Business Group on Health (PBGH). PBGH, a nonprofit coalition of forty-eight major California employers that oversees the health-care purchasing for approximately 3 million employees, retirees, and their families and nearly $4 billion in annual health-care expenses, is nationally recognized for its efforts to improve the quality and availability of health care while moderating costs. PBGH makes HealthScope available on the Internet to anyone free of charge. To create HealthScope, PBGH conducted its own surveys, as well as analyzed data collected by the state of California on individuals hospitalized with cardiac and other illnesses. HealthScope helps individuals answer questions such as the following:

- Will my health plan give me access to high-quality medical groups and doctors?
- How do I find hospitals that produce better results for their patients?
- How easy is it to get an O.K. to see the specialists I may need?
- How satisfied are other consumers with a particular health plan, medical group, or hospital?
- Does my doctor's medical group quickly see patients who need care?
- Does the health plan see that patients get treatment that has been proven to work?

making of different types of report cards. We would also emphasize research that seeks to measure the extent to which compensating doctors, hospitals, and insurers on the basis of report cards enhances their utility to consumers.

Second, we propose that HHS improve its efforts to encourage use of generally recommended treatments through the development and dissemination of guidelines, keeping in mind that while guidelines can help practicing physicians make use of the most recent scientific research, blind adherence to them runs the risk of one-size-fits-all medicine.

The surgeon general can help to make guidelines easier for physicians and patients to use. More accessible guidelines not only serve to inform physicians of best practices, but they also alert patients to the onset of illness and encourage them to become more involved in their health-care decisions. We propose that the surgeon general, in consultation with HHS, physician organizations, state health departments, and insurers, identify the most costly and prevalent illnesses whose generally accepted best practices are not universally followed, post these illnesses with their respective guidelines on the Internet, and undertake a public-service campaign to increase patient and physician compliance.

Control Anticompetitive Behavior

As with the functioning of insurance markets, we also have many of the tools necessary to control private anticompetitive behavior. American antitrust laws have protected consumers and promoted free markets that have made the U.S. economy the strongest in the world. We have already proposed that the exemption from antitrust laws for insurers under the McCarran-Ferguson Act be sharply limited. In addition, public policy can take further steps to ensure competitive health-care markets. Three practices should receive top priority from the antitrust enforcement agencies.

First, we propose aggressive investigation of mergers among hospitals that lead to very high concentrations of market power. Recent research shows that such concentrations both raise costs and reduce quality.[32] For Medicare beneficiaries suffering from heart attack, the costs of care in the most competitive areas were approximately 8 percent lower than those in the least competitive areas, and mortality after one year approximately 4 percent lower.[33] When doctors and their patients lack choices, hospitals lose the incentive to provide effective and efficient care.

Second, we propose to limit strictly the ability of doctors and hospitals to boycott patients and their health plans in order to obtain anticompetitive concessions on prices and quality. Many believe that allowing doctors and hospitals the latitude to join together against health plans will only affect the health plans' profits, not costs for consumers. They are mistaken. Increases in prices and health-care costs translate into higher premiums for firms and workers, rising rates of uninsurance, and higher costs for the Medicare and Medicaid programs.

Third, we propose exploration of the existence and potential effects of barriers to the entry into the field of new physicians and specialists. The Accreditation Council for Graduate

Medical Education (ACGME), a private organization controlled by physicians and hospitals, exercises virtually complete control in every specialty over the number of residency programs and the number of residents in each program—and therefore over the flow of new physicians.[34] In any other industry, an agreement by participants to limit entry of new competitors would be considered a violation of the antitrust laws; why should health care be different? Graduate medical education must be subject to rigorous quality controls, but this goal can be accomplished without the anticompetitive effects of the ACGME's current approach.

Reform the Malpractice System

Research on medical malpractice litigation by both academics and government agencies is clear: The broken litigation system leads to fewer choices for patients and to higher costs because of "defensive medicine." As a first step to reforming the malpractice system, we propose reasonable, national caps on noneconomic damages in medical malpractice lawsuits. Doctors in Nevada, Pennsylvania, Mississippi, North Carolina, Virginia, Florida, Ohio, and Illinois—all states without reasonable limits on noneconomic damages— had recent annual increases in their malpractice premiums of between 30 and 75 percent.

Evidence that these increases have led to decreases in physician availability, particularly among specialists, is persuasive. Two recent studies report that states adopting reforms that directly reduce liability, such as caps on noneconomic damages, experienced significantly greater growth in physicians per capita over the 1980s and 1990s than states without such caps.[35]

In addition to fewer choices, malpractice pressure leads to higher health-care costs beyond its direct impact on malpractice insurance. Not only do doctors and hospitals pass on the direct costs of increased malpractice premiums, they provide more expensive and relatively unproductive medical treatments out of fear of litigation. The additional cost of defensive medicine attributable to the medical liability system is estimated to range from 3 to 7 percent (box 8).[36]

Three alternative reforms to the tort system also hold significant promise. First, systems of error-reporting, analysis, and feedback—which are central to efforts to reduce medical errors—should be protected from liability. The most important impediment to the creation and success of these systems is the discoverability of their data by potential plaintiffs in medical malpractice lawsuits. States differ in the extent to which they protect analyses of medical errors by hospitals, physician groups, and insurers from lawsuits. Such analyses are generally discoverable by plaintiffs, unless the analysis falls under a state's specific statutory exception.[37] However, even states with these statutory exceptions do not generally protect information that is shared across organizations.

Consistent with findings of the Institute of Medicine[38] and many bills that have been introduced in Congress, we

Box 8

THE COSTS OF DEFENSIVE MEDICINE

How costly is defensive medicine, and how effective are legal reforms at reducing its prevalence? To investigate this question, Daniel Kessler and Mark McClellan analyzed longitudinal data on essentially all elderly Medicare beneficiaries hospitalized with serious cardiac illness from 1984 to 1994, matched with information on the medical malpractice liability reforms in effect in the state in which each patient was treated.[39] They modeled the effect of reforms on total hospital expenditures on the patient in the year after the onset of illness and on important patient outcomes, and they estimated the effect of reforms on a serious adverse outcome that is common in our study population: mortality within one year of occurrence of the cardiac illness. They also estimated the effect of reforms on two other common adverse outcomes related to a patient's quality of life—whether the patient experienced a subsequent heart attack or heart failure requiring hospitalization in the year following the initial illness. They compared trends in treatments, costs, and outcomes for patients from states reforming their liability system to patients from nonreforming states, holding constant patient background characteristics, state, and time-fixed effects, and the legal and political characteristics of states.

Kessler and McClellan's analysis indicated that reforms that directly limited liability—such as caps on damages—reduced hospital expenditures by 3–7 percent, depending on the type of patient and the market

(continued on next page)

(Box 8, *continued*)

environment. In contrast, reforms that limited liability only indirectly were not associated with any substantial expenditure effects. Neither type of reform led to any consequential differences in mortality or the occurrence of serious complications. Thus, treatment of elderly patients with heart disease does involve defensive medical practices, and limited reductions in liability can reduce this costly behavior.

propose to limit the discoverability of data on adverse events collected for purposes of quality improvement. Such legal protection will encourage health-care organizations to develop policies to collect and analyze information about medical errors and encourage health-care workers to report mistakes. Passing such legislation would be an important step toward reducing medical errors.

Second, patients and providers should be given more freedom to experiment with alternatives to the courts. In binding alternative dispute resolution (ADR), patients and providers voluntarily submit disputes to an arbitrator who resolves the case in a binding decision. According to its proponents, ADR compensates victims faster, more fairly, and with lower transaction costs. ADR also can enhance the incentives for doctors and hospitals to take more appropriate precautions against medical errors, by replacing the current compensation lottery with a more consistent decision-making process.[40]

Yet ADR is surprisingly uncommon. Its proponents argue that state laws and judicial decisions that make ADR agreements impossible to enforce leave arbitrators powerless. According to this reasoning, few agree to ADR because its decisions do not mean much. Opponents of ADR argue that bias in favor of defendants, or at least the perception of bias, is responsible for its unpopularity. According to this reasoning, patients are wary of ADR because arbitrators are more likely to develop ties to the provider organizations that pay for their services than to individual plaintiffs.

Before we give up on ADR, we need to reform public policy to give it a chance. To give everyone more confidence in ADR, legal and regulatory reform should ensure that its decisions are both enforceable and impartial.

Third, we propose to study adoption of a guidelines-based rule for adjudicating physician negligence in malpractice claims. Under the common law of most states, physician negligence is an issue of fact for the jury, informed by expert testimony. Under a guidelines-based system, compliance with a guideline could be allowed as a defense to malpractice; failure to comply with a guideline, without a patient's written permission, could be allowed as evidence of malpractice. Although guidelines are an obvious source of information about the negligence of a given treatment decision in a medical malpractice case, courts generally bar them from being admitted as evidence under the hearsay rule, which prohibits the introduction of out-of-court statements as evidence. Guidelines are sometimes admitted under the "learned treatise" exception to the hearsay rule. Under most states' common law, no one set of guidelines necessarily trumps any other, and they carry no more weight than any other form of expert testimony.[41] Thus, adoption of a guidelines-based system would require legislative action.

Several states have already experimented with legal reforms that make evidence of compliance with guidelines statutorily admissible by defendants as an affirmative defense to malpractice. For example, Florida and Maine passed laws creating demonstration projects in the 1990s that allowed physicians to opt into a guidelines-based malpractice system.[42] Because there are many contexts in which medical care is widely known to deviate from "best practices," expanding the role of guidelines has the potential to improve the quality of care further.

Study the Tax Preference for Nonprofits

Finally, we propose that the U.S. Department of Treasury and Department of Health and Human Services study whether current government policy governing the tax exemption for not-for-profit health-care institutions is in the public interest. First, the empirical evidence about the exemption's effectiveness as a vehicle for promoting care for the poor is equivocal at best (see box 9). Second, to the extent that our proposed policy package increases insurance-coverage rates, tax subsidies for uncompensated care

Box 9

THE CONSEQUENCES OF FOR-PROFIT VERSUS NONPROFIT OWNERSHIP OF HOSPITALS

Economists and health-policy scholars have long been interested in three potential consequences of for-profit versus nonprofit ownership of hospitals: the effect of ownership on the magnitude of benefits supplied to the community, the effect on productive efficiency, and the effect on tax revenues.

Most studies have found essentially no difference in the community benefits provided by for-profit versus nonprofit hospitals, where community benefits are defined to include uncompensated care and the provision of unprofitable or nonreimbursable services.[43] Indeed, some studies find that nonprofits actually treat fewer indigent patients than for-profits.[44] There is some evidence that public hospitals that convert to for-profit status reduce the amount of uncompensated care they supply. However, public hospitals that convert supply much lower levels of uncompensated care before their conversion than public hospitals that do not convert.[45]

Evidence on the prices and/or costs of for-profit versus nonprofit hospitals is slightly more mixed. Some older studies find that for-profits have higher prices and/or costs, but more recent work suggests that these differences have shrunk or even reversed themselves.[46] There is also evidence that the presence of for-profits in an area leads to more efficient production of hospital services—even by nonprofits.[47]

A recent study calculated the revenue cost of the tax subsidy provided to nonprofit hospitals and found that in

(continued on next page)

(Box 9, *continued*)

1994–95 it amounted to $9.21 billion in 2002 dollars, including an exemption from income taxes of $5.43 billion, an exemption from property taxes of $2.01 billion, tax deductibility of donor contributions of $1.34 billion, and tax-exemption of interest paid on debt of $0.43 billion.[48]

become less necessary. Third, the tax exemption protects nonprofit institutions from competition from for-profit institutions, thereby lessening the competitive pressures to make nonprofits as efficient as possible. Finally, the revenue gained from removing the tax exemption for nonprofits could be used to finance other improvements in health-care coverage and treatment.

3

Impacts of Proposals on Health-Care Spending, the Uninsured, the Federal Budget, and the Distribution of Tax Burdens

The U.S. health-care system remains the finest in the world, leading in innovation and quality of care. At the same time, increasing failures in the workings of markets for health insurance and health care have fostered concerns that the system is too costly for all Americans and unavailable to some. The combination of third-party payment for most health care, weak incentives for consumers and producers, and a growing presence of government in health-care financing spells trouble, both in terms of value and access today and stifled innovation in the future. The alternative is to alter incentives for consumers and providers in private health-care markets.

We have proposed policy changes to empower consumers and improve competition and choice in health-care markets. These changes are incremental—they can be implemented in most cases with simple modifications of existing law—but they set forth a powerful new policy direction by promoting true health insurance, making consumers better-informed purchasers of health care, and enhancing competition in health-insurance and health-care markets. The changes share a common goal—improving the ability of private markets to insure and provide health care—thereby benefiting Americans today through lower costs and greater choice, and Americans in the future by providing the best incentives for capturing the innovative possibilities in health care in this century.

The steps we have outlined offer two significant potential gains: a reduction in the resources spent on relatively unproductive care, and a reduction in the number of uninsured.

Effects of Reforms on Health-Care Spending

In this section, we summarize the effects of four of our policy reforms on health-care spending: tax deductibility, the tax credit, insurance-market reforms, and malpractice reforms. (These effects are listed in box 10.) In each case, we use estimates of the magnitude of behavioral responses from the existing academic literature. A more complete description of these behavioral responses and how they were used to obtain estimated impacts is provided in the appendices. We assume that health-care subsidies for the chronically ill will have no impact on health spending and will primarily shift health-care expenditures from inefficient financing through health-insurance regulation to direct subsidies.

Box 10

IMPACT OF PROPOSALS ON HEALTH-CARE SPENDING

	Percent Change	Absolute Change ($ billion)
Tax Deductibility	−6.2	−43
Tax Credit	−	1
Insurance-Market Reforms	−1.0	−7
Medical Malprac- tice Reform	−1.7	−12
Total	**−8.9**	**−61**

SOURCE: Authors' calculations.

Tax Deductibility. We begin with the impact of tax deductibility. Allowing out-of-pocket health-care spending to be tax deductible has two opposing effects on health-care spending. First, expanding deductibility lowers the overall price of health care relative to other goods and services and, thereby, increases spending. Second, expanding deductibility raises the price of purchasing health care through insurance relative to out-of-pocket. The second effect induces people to shift to health plans with higher deductibles and coinsurance rates, which, in turn, lowers spending.

Our key result is that the expenditure-reducing effect of full deductibility is greater in magnitude than the expenditure-increasing effect. We are not the first researchers to recognize this possibility.[1] This result is important for two reasons. First, it implies that full deductibility is an effective policy to address rising health-care costs. Second, it has important implications for the policy's impact on the federal budget. Reductions in health-care expenditures that come from removing the tax-favored status of health insurance are not a loss to the economy; that is, GDP will not decline by the reduction in health-care spending. The tax-free resources no longer used for health-care consumption will be channeled to other, taxable, economic activities. The resulting increase in tax revenues will offset a significant amount of the loss from making out-of-pocket health-care expenditures tax deductible.

We calculate the total effect of deductibility in two steps. First, we calculate the extent to which full deductibility would reduce the after-tax price of out-of-pocket spending. Across all taxpayers, we estimate that this price would decline by about 15 percent. Second, we calculate the responsiveness of total health expenditures to a decrease in this price. Based on estimates from the literature, we calculate that each 1 percent decrease in the after-tax price of out-of-pocket expenditure would reduce total health expenditures (on insurance and out of pocket) by 0.41 percent (see appendix A). Hence, full deductibility would reduce health-care spending by 6.2 percent (= 0.41 x 15 percent).

This savings of approximately 6 percent in private health spending would translate into modestly higher coinsurance rates and dramatically lower expenditures on health insurance. A 6.2 percent reduction amounts to a $43 billion reduction in aggregate U.S. private health-care spending in 2004. In appendix B we show that if this reduction were achieved entirely through a rise in coinsurance rates, the typical coin-surance rate would rise from 25 to 35 percent.

Tax Credit. Implementation of the health-care tax credit would raise overall health-care spending as each newly insured recipient increased his use of health-care services. We estimate that the tax credit would increase the number of insured individuals by 5 million. If each newly insured person increased his spending by 27 percent, aggregate U.S. health-care spending would rise by about $1 billion per year. Thus, increases in health-care spending due to the tax credit would offset the $43 billion decline due to deductibility, but only by a small amount (see appendix C for calculations).

Insurance-Market Reform. In our previous discussion of insurance-market reforms, we noted that the Congressional Budget Office had estimated that eliminating state benefit mandates alone would reduce the cost of a typical insurance plan by 5 percent and possibly as much as 15 percent.[2] Similarly, eliminating any-willing-provider laws would reduce the cost of insurance by nearly 2 percent.[3]

Based upon the lower end of the range of estimates by the Congressional Budget Office, our proposed insurance reforms would reduce the cost of insurance by 7 percent. Because individuals would respond to lower insurance costs by increasing their insured expenditures, we estimate that insurance-market reforms would reduce health-care spend-ing by only 1 percent, or $7 billion per year (appendix A).

Malpractice Reform. In our previous discussion of malpractice reforms, we reported that the additional cost of defensive medicine attributable to the medical liability system is estimated to be in the range of 3–7 percent. We assume that limits on noneconomic damages would reduce the overall cost of care by the lower end of this range, 3 percent. Allowing for individuals to respond to this reduction by increasing their purchases of care would reduce the impact to 1.7 percent, or $12 billion per year (appendix A).

Summary and Discussion. Taken together, the four proposals discussed here would reduce total health-care spending by 8.9 percent, or $61 billion per year.

The most common criticisms of our proposals are of two types: that our expenditure savings depends upon unrealistic estimates of the effect of the responsiveness of health spending to copayment rates; and that higher copayment rates will not have much effect on the bulk of medical expenditures, which are incurred by the chronically or terminally ill. In our view, neither of these criticisms is strong.

First, calculations of the overall impact of our policies on spending are not sensitive to the magnitude of the response of health spending to its effective price. Even if individuals' behavioral response is half as great as we assume it is, the total effect of our package on health spending would be 9.4 percent—greater than our estimate of 8.9 percent. The composition of savings would shift from being primarily due to deductibility to being due about equally to deductibility, insurance-market reform, and malpractice reform (see appendix A for details); but the bottom-line total would be roughly the same.

Second, health insurance based on health savings accounts combined with a catastrophic plan can, in practice, subject most expenditures to the discipline of "spending your own money." Two common arguments against this proposition—the high persistence of expenditures and the high cost of end-of-life care—are far weaker than they are commonly believed to be. Matthew Eichner, Mark McClellan, and David Wise analyzed the health-insurance claims of a large Fortune 500 manufacturing company from 1989 to 1991.[4] They report that among employees ages forty-six to fifty-five with health expenditures of at least $5,000 in 1989 (roughly the top decile of spenders), only 28.6 percent had expenditures of at least $5,000 in 1990.[5] Alan Monheit's analysis of the data from the Medical Expenditure Panel Survey finds persistence that is somewhat greater, not substantially so.[6] Among individuals in the top decile of spenders in 1996, 37.9 percent remained in the top decile in 1997.[7]

Although the cost of end-of-life care is not trivial, the share of Medicare expenditures incurred in the last year of life has remained roughly constant over the past twenty years at one-quarter of the total.[8] Thus, even if higher deductibles and copayments could not affect the cost of care at the end of life, they could still affect three-quarters of the level—and growth—in expenditures. In addition, there is evidence that the same incentives that affect the cost of care of chronically ill survivors also affect the care of chronically ill decedents. It is generally not possible to predict individual patient mortality with sufficient specificity to influence medical decision making, even with detailed clinical records: The characteristics of Medicare decedents are similar to those of high-cost survivors.[9]

Effects of Reforms on the Uninsured

We have developed a four-pronged policy to reduce the number of uninsured persons: full above-the-line tax deductibility of both insurance premiums and out-of-pocket expenses; tax credits; and malpractice and insurance-market reforms to make health insurance more affordable, more portable, and better tailored to individuals' needs.

Tax Deductibility. Full tax deductibility would decrease the price of insurance for a large number of uninsured persons. Based on calculations using the Medical Expenditure Panel Survey, we estimate that nearly half (46 percent) of the 43 million nonelderly, uninsured individuals (about 20 million) would benefit from tax deductibility, and between 2 and 6 million would be induced to purchase insurance (see appendix C for details).

Tax Credit. The tax credit would further reduce the number of uninsured. According to data from the Medical Expenditure Panel Survey, one in every five nonelderly uninsured individuals is in a household earning less than the poverty threshold, and nearly half are in households earning 100–300 percent of the poverty threshold. How many of these 30 million persons would be induced to purchase health insurance as a consequence of the tax credit is subject to considerable empirical uncertainty. Using estimates from Mark Pauly and Bradley Herring, we estimate that between two and seven million individuals would do so (see appendix C).

Insurance-Market and Malpractice Reforms. Allowing insurance companies to sell policies free from state benefit-mandates and any-willing-provider laws on a nationwide basis would be to reduce costs by approximately 7 percent;[10] malpractice reforms would produce a 3 percent reduction. In addition, our reforms would make insurance more portable and therefore more attractive, holding price constant. We estimate that the insurance-market and malpractice reforms would reduce the number of uninsured by between 2 and 7 million individuals (see appendix C).

Summary and Discussion. Taken together, our proposed policy changes are projected to reduce the number of uninsured persons by 6 to 20 million. The impact of these proposals on the ranks of uninsured, while substantial in their own right, might be even greater than these calculations suggest. For example, the more than 14 million uninsured Americans who are eligible for—but not enrolled in—government programs like Medicaid and/or SCHIP could also benefit from a more viable individual market, because Medicaid and SCHIP waivers can redirect existing (unused) funds into insurance vehicles to cover these individuals.

In addition, our policies are unlikely to increase the number of uninsured by inducing employers to stop offering health insurance to their employees. Our policy of full deductibility retains a significant tax incentive for purchase of employer-provided insurance, so that any transition to a new mix of individual versus employer-sponsored insurance would be gradual. In particular, our proposal only allows the deduction of the cost of individual insurance from the income-tax base, not from the payroll-tax base. Expenditures on insurance purchased through an employer would, as under current law, still be excludable from both the income- and payroll-tax bases.

However, existing empirical evidence suggests that even if the after-tax prices of individual insurance and employer-provided insurance were fully equalized, employers' dropping of insurance would not be commonplace. Even in the absence of any tax preference, employers would only cease to offer insurance if their workers' demands for insurance were so different that the gains to low-demand workers from buying less insurance in the individual market outweighed the loss to all workers of the individual market's higher administrative costs. Research by Mark Pauly, Allison Percy, and Bradley Herring shows that this is unlikely to be the case. Under plausible assumptions about the extent of the differences in employees' demand for insurance at a typical firm, they report that the average benefit to an employee of opting out of his employer-provided insurance plan (in the absence of any tax preference) is approximately equal to the average cost, in terms of the increased administrative expenses that he would face in the individual versus the group-insurance market.[11]

Effects of Reforms on the Federal Budget

We now present the federal budget impact of our main policy reforms. For purposes of calculation, these include the four reforms mentioned above—tax deductibility, the tax credit, and insurance-market and malpractice reforms—plus health-care subsidies for the chronically ill.

Tax Deductibility. Deductibility of health-care expenses would have three effects on the federal budget: the revenue loss from making currently taxed health expenditures tax-deductible; the revenue gain from the shift in health-care spending from employer-provided insurance (which is currently free from both income and payroll taxes) to out-of-pocket (which would be free only from income taxes); and the revenue gain from the reduction in spending through employer-provided insurance (which was free from income and payroll taxes, and would become fully taxable).

Tax deductibility would create a revenue loss by making currently taxed health spending deductible. Currently, after-tax payments for health care consist of two components: out-of-pocket payments for the direct purchase of medical care, and individual after-tax premium payments for health insurance. According to our calculations, these two forms of currently taxed health-care payments total $191 billion. Making them tax-deductible would create a federal revenue loss of $28 billion per year (see appendix E).

Tax deductibility would also lead to a shift in how medical care is purchased, away from insurance and toward out-of-pocket expenses, and a reduction in overall spending. Earlier, we estimated that tax deductibility would cause private employer-provided health-insurance expenditures to decline by about 22 percent, or about $110 billion per year. Workers would spend a portion of these increased wages on higher out-of-pocket health-care payments and individual health insurance, both of which would be deductible from income taxes but subject to payroll taxes. The remainder would be channeled into higher wages to workers. Just as increases in health-insurance costs are borne by workers in the form of lower wages, decreases would accrue to them as higher wages, which would be subject to both payroll and income taxes.

We estimate that the redirection of expenditures on employer-provided insurance to out-of-pocket spending and taxable wages would result in a net increase in revenues to the federal government of $22 billion per year (see appendix E). At first glance, this estimate may seem large. When considered relative to the impact of the tax exclusion, however, it appears less so. For example, in 2004, the health-insurance tax exclusion reduced federal revenue by an estimated $189 billion.[12] The changes in health-care policy that would be generated by our proposals, but mainly by tax deductibility, would offset less than 20 percent of this loss.

Combining the estimates of the revenue losses and gains from tax deductibility, we estimate its net impact to be a revenue loss of $6 billion.

Tax Credit. The revenue loss from the tax credit is the sum of two components—the cost from the use of the credit by currently insured individuals, and the cost from its use by newly insured individuals. The credit's use by currently insured persons would cost the treasury $3 billion in annual revenues, and its use by newly insured persons would cost another $2 billion (see appendix E for details).

Insurance-Market and Malpractice Reforms. We estimate that insurance-market and malpractice reforms would reduce overall health spending by 2.7 percent, or $19 billion. This transfer of health spending to other economic activities would be subject to both income and payroll taxation and generate a $5 billion increase in annual federal revenues.

Subsidy for the Chronically Ill. The revenue loss from our proposal to provide federal subsidies for the chronically ill would depend upon three key parameters: the number of eligible people who take up the subsidy, the average health-care costs of an eligible person, and the generosity of the subsidy. We do not recommend a particular set of policy parameters at this juncture; instead, we offer an example for purposes of illustration.

In our example, we assume our proposed subsidy would cover approximately one-third more people than are currently

---

Box 11

IMPACT OF PROPOSED POLICIES ON FEDERAL REVENUES

	Annual Revenue Impact
Tax Deductibility	−$6 billion
Tax Credit	−$5 billion
Insurance-Market and Malpractice Reforms	$5 billion
Subsidy for the Chronically Ill	−$3 billion
Total	**−$9 billion**

SOURCE: Authors' calculations.

---

covered by all state high-risk pools together, or 140,000 people.[13] This difference would amount to approximately 1 percent of the estimated number of people who would purchase insurance in the new federal market. (We base our estimate of the initial size of the federal market on the number of nonelderly people in 2002 with private health insurance not obtained through their employer or a relative's employer—16,504,000.)[14]

We assume an average cost per person of the subsidy of $23,640, and we estimate the average level of health expenditures for an eligible person to be $46,520, equal to the average cost per person of the most costly 1 percent of the population insured by Anthem, a large health insurer.[15] For purposes of this example, we further assume that the subsidy would cover 75 percent of the expenses of an eligible person in excess of $15,000. Thus, in this example, we estimate the annual cost of the subsidy to be $23,640 x 140,000, or $3 billion.

Box 11 summarizes the total impact of our proposed policy changes on the federal budget.

Distributional Impact

We compute two measures of the distributional impact of our tax policies using data from the 2002 Medical Expenditure Panel Survey. The first measure is the percentage reduction in each income group's taxes that results solely from tax deductibility (see figure 4); the second measure is the same reduction when the credit is included (see figure 5). We estimate the distributional effects of the credit under the (very conservative) assumption that no individuals become newly insured due to the credit. Assuming no change in the income distribution, these measures are equal to the percentage change in tax burden as a share of income.

As figure 4 shows, the policy of making health-care expenses tax-deductible is by itself progressive. Percentage tax reductions for low-income households are three to five times the same reductions for high-income households. For example, households earning less than $20,000 per year can expect a 5.7 percent reduction in their average tax rate, while households earning from $20,000 to $30,000 per year can expect an 8.3 percent reduction. This reduction comes about because our policy allows health expenses to be deducted "above the line"—that is, even by nonitemizing taxpayers. By comparison, households earning from $70,000 to $100,000 per year can expect only a 1.8 percent reduction in their average tax rate, and households earning more than $100,000 a 1 percent reduction.

As figure 5 shows, full deductibility combined with the tax credit is even more progressive. Households earning less

FIGURE 4

PERCENTAGE TAX REDUCTION: FULL TAX DEDUCTIBILITY PROPOSAL

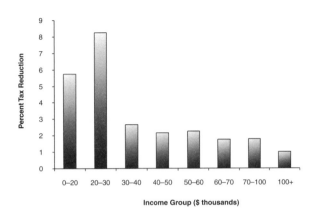

SOURCE: Authors' calculations.

FIGURE 5

PERCENTAGE TAX REDUCTION: TAX DEDUCTIBILITY AND TAX CREDIT

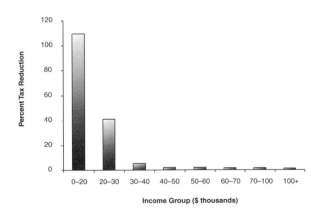

SOURCE: Authors' calculations.

than $20,000 per year can expect a 110 percent reduction in their average tax rate; households earning $20,000–$30,000 per year can expect a 41 percent reduction.

Conclusion

The U.S. health-care system, the envy of the world in innovation, faces significant criticisms about the cost, accessibility, and quality of care. While these criticisms are not without foundation, a more productive approach is to ask whether consumers of health care—and taxpayers in public financing—are obtaining the highest "value" for the resources devoted to health care. That is, are we getting what we should in return for the investments that we make, as individuals and a society, in our health care?

In our view, achieving this objective stands the greatest chance of success if health-care markets function well. Market-based reform is neither a silver bullet nor a cure-all. Markets will not eliminate growth in health-care costs—an inevitable product of technological change—or uninsurance. Markets will never solve the problem of how to finance care for the low-income chronically ill. But the power of markets to allocate resources efficiently—power evident in every other sector of the economy—is part of the solution.

Yet markets cannot flourish without the appropriate institutional support for consumer incentives and choice, provider accountability, and competition. These needed features are held back in the United States in substantial measure by the unintended consequences of public policies in five areas. Any serious reform of the U.S. health-care system must begin by changing these policies.

In two areas, public policy has actively hindered the operation of markets for health services. First, and most important, is the tax preference for employer-provided health insurance. Current tax policy generally allows people to deduct employer-provided health-insurance expenditures, but requires direct out-of-pocket medical spending to be made from after-tax income. This tax preference has given consumers the incentive to purchase health care through low-deductible, low-copayment insurance instead of out-of-pocket. This type of insurance has led to today's U.S. health-care market in which cost unconsciousness and wasteful medical practices are the norm. The reason is, as Milton Friedman put it, "Nobody spends somebody else's money as wisely as he spends his own."[1]

The best way to reverse this trend would be to revoke the tax preference. Unfortunately, as experience from the tax-reform debates of the 1980s showed, this solution appears politically infeasible. We propose a second-best solution: Allow all Americans to deduct expenditures on health insurance and out-of-pocket expenses as long as they purchase at least catastrophic insurance. We show that under reasonable assumptions, expanding deductibility to out-of-pocket expenses will lead to a dramatic reduction in minimally productive health spending.

We are not the first researchers to recognize this possibility. Many economists and health-services researchers have recognized that expanding deductibility has two opposing effects on health-care spending. First, it lowers the overall price of health care relative to other goods and services and, thereby, increases health-care spending. Second, it raises the price of purchasing health care through insurance relative to out-of-pocket. The second effect induces people to shift to health plans with higher deductibles and coinsurance rates, which, in turn, lowers health-care spending. Because the base of out-of-pocket spending is so much smaller than that of insured spending, the net change in the *overall* price of health care from expanding deductibility is much smaller than the change in the *relative* price of out-of-pocket versus insured care. This fact leads the second effect to dominate the first and, in turn, to a net decrease in spending.

Expanding deductibility will have numerous other beneficial effects. Most notably, it will unambiguously reduce the rate of uninsurance. The most important cause of uninsurance is the high cost of health care; as we show, full deductibility significantly reduces the net cost of care for many of the uninsured, even those with moderate incomes. In addition, because the tax change allows the deductibility of out-of-pocket health-care expenses only with the purchase of insurance, it creates a significant incentive for the currently uninsured to purchase insurance. Because it allows the deduction of the cost of individual insurance from the income-tax base but not from the payroll-tax base, the change retains a significant tax incentive for the purchase of employer-sponsored insurance as well. Expenditures on insurance purchased through an employer would, as under current law, still be excludable from both the income- and the payroll-tax base.

The tax change also enhances the fairness of the federal income-tax system. Under current law, individuals whose employers decline to offer them insurance are penalized because they must purchase it with after-tax income. Tax deductibility would promote tax simplicity by replacing the myriad of currently available special health-care tax deductions discussed above with a single deduction equally applicable to all individuals. Finally, deductibility would increase the progressivity of the tax system. Although marginal tax rates are higher for higher-income people, the fact that lower-income people have higher (currently taxable) out-of-pocket spending more than compensates for this effect.

We combine the policy of full deductibility with other important changes to federal tax policy. To make it easier for individuals and families to save for expenses not covered by higher-deductible insurance, we propose allowing all individuals to contribute $1,000 per year ($2,000 maximum per household) to a health savings account, conditional on the purchase of insurance that covers at least catastrophic expenditures. As with current HSAs, balances may be spent on the health care of a relative, and those not spent on health care could be carried forward tax free. Funds withdrawn for purposes other than health care would be subject to income tax. Recipients of health-care tax credits (described below) could deposit funds in a health savings account if they wish. The purpose of these proposed changes is to make the current law governing HSAs less prescriptive and, thereby, encourage greater use of HSAs. To improve the health-care "safety net" for very-low-income households, we propose a refundable tax credit to offset their health expenses. While our proposal to make out-of-pocket medical expenses tax-deductible offers important benefits for many low- and middle-income working families, it does not help families that pay little or no income tax.

The second area in need of policy reform is the regulation of markets for health insurance. Like the tax preference, the unintended consequences of inefficient insurance regulation are to drive up costs and increase uninsurance. We propose that insurance companies that meet certain federal standards be permitted to offer plans on a nationwide basis free from costly state mandates, rules, and regulations. With this change, insurance would become available to individuals and small groups on the same terms and conditions as those currently available to employees of many large corporations who, because of a quirk in federal law, have been exempt from state insurance regulations for more than thirty years.

Given that approximately half of the insured U.S. population already obtains its insurance in what is effectively a federal market, this reform will not lead to radical or unpredictable changes in consumer protections. Federally certified health-insurance products would be required to meet all federal regulations that currently govern the provision of health insurance for large employers; there would be no rollback of existing federal health-insurance protections. Insurance companies that offer federally certified products would be required to meet financial structure and solvency requirements. In addition, states could continue to supervise day-to-day market conduct. Finally, insurance companies that offer federally certified products would no longer be exempt from federal antitrust statutes under the McCarran-Ferguson Act.

There are several benefits to creating a federally certified market for health insurance. Most importantly, this change will foster a more competitive, efficient, nongroup health-insurance market that will enable individuals to obtain a greater variety of lower-cost alternatives. The lower cost will induce more people to buy insurance and, thereby, increase the size of risk pools—which will, in turn, further strengthen markets for insurance. In addition, a federal market will increase the portability of health insurance by making it easier for people to keep their insurance when they move across state lines.

Regulation of markets for insurance can be improved in another important way. To help competitive insurance markets provide affordable insurance for people with predictably high medical expenses year after year who lack sufficient resources to finance them, we propose making such people eligible for a subsidy to purchase insurance in the new nationwide market. A public-private partnership between the federal government and insurance companies would administer the subsidy. To be eligible, chronically ill persons would have to have been covered by insurance in the past and have insufficient resources to pay for their own coverage. Previous research has shown that states' current responses to the problem of the chronically ill—high-risk pools and insurance-rate regulation—have not addressed this important health policy problem. A targeted subsidy to those who are needy and suffering from insurance-market failure would provide a far more cost-effective solution.

We also propose reforms in three additional areas: better provision of information to providers and consumers; an explicit public goal to control anticompetitive behavior by doctors, hospitals, and insurers; and reforms to the malpractice system to reduce wasteful treatment and medical errors. In each of these areas, research has indicated significant opportunities to achieve improvements in medical productivity that exceed the cost of the reforms.

Taken together, these changes harness the power of markets for health insurance and health care to deliver higher-value health care to Americans. They also allow markets to focus insurance and care arrangements more on individual needs. And better incentives promote consumers' ability to be cost- and value-conscious shoppers, as well as providers' accountability for quality and innovation in therapies, drugs, and medical devices. While the sweep of the reforms is radical, each change can be implemented as an incremental reform of the present U.S. health-care system.

The time to implement these reforms is now. Failure to do so will exacerbate the problems of wasteful cost growth and uninsurance, while increasing the pressure for more public intervention, with adverse consequences for innovation and flexibility. With this stark choice, health care is likely to be the center stage of domestic policy debates over the next decade.

Box 12

The Effects of the Five Policy Reforms

1. Health-Care Tax Reform
   - Total deductibility of health-care expenses
   - Expanded health savings accounts
   - Tax credits for low-income individuals and families

Impact: Lower the cost of insurance; level the playing field between employer-provided and individual insurance; promote catastrophic coverage by leveling the playing field between out-of-pocket expenses and insurance costs.

2. Insurance Reform
   - Nationwide portable health insurance
   - Subsidized private insurance for the chronically ill

Impact: Reduce insurance costs and promote insurance coverage and portability.

3. Improve Health Information
   - Expand number and scope of report cards on doctors and hospitals
   - Promote use of "best practices" through guidelines

Impact: Make better shoppers and improve the performance of doctors and hospitals.

4. Control Anticompetitive Behavior by Providers and Insurers
5. Reform the Malpractice System and Study the Tax Preference for Nonprofits

Impact: Lower costs of care; increase insurance coverage; reduce medical errors.

Net Impact:
- **6–20 million more insured Americans**
- **9 percent reduction in health-care expenditures**

Estimating the Impact of Policy Reforms on Health-Care Spending

We estimated the effect of deductibility on health-care spending in two steps. First, we calculated a weighted-average marginal tax rate for all households, using each household's reported out-of-pocket expenses, including direct payments for health insurance by households without a self-employed person, as the weights. To do this, we used household-level data from the 2002 Medical Expenditure Panel Survey (MEPS), and inflated expenditures to 2004 levels using the Medical Consumer Price Index (MCPI).[1] We imputed a federal 2004 income-tax rate based upon the household's reported income and estimated tax deductions. We calculated a weighted-average marginal tax rate for all households, using each household's reported out-of-pocket expenses, including direct payments for health insurance by non–self-employed households, as the weights. We conclude that full deductibility would reduce the price of out-of-pocket health care relative to all other goods and services by 14 percent. Evaluated at the average after-tax price, this amounts to a 15 percent decrease $(= 0.14p_i / ((p_i + (p_i - 0.14p_i)) / 2)$, where p_i is the before-tax price of insured expenditures).

Second, we calculated the effect on total health expenditures of a 1 percent increase in the after-tax price of out-of-pocket expenditures, as a function of the effect on total health expenditures of a 1 percent increase in the overall price of health care and the effect on total health expenditures of a 1 percent increase in the after-tax price of insured expenditures. This formula can be written:

$$e(t_o) \approx e(p) - e(t_i),$$

where $e(t_o)$ is the effect on total health expenditures of a 1 percent increase in the after-tax price of out-of-pocket expenditures; $e(p)$ is the effect on total health expenditures of a 1 percent increase in the overall price of health care; and $e(t_i)$ is the effect on total health expenditures of a 1 percent increase in the after-tax price of insured expenditures. (The proof of this proposition is in appendix D.)

Both $e(p)$ and $e(t_i)$ are negative. Increases in the overall price of health care will lead to decreases in total expenditures; increases in the after-tax price of insured expenditures will lead to decreases in total expenditures as well. The effect on total expenditures of the after-tax price of insured expenditures consists of two components that work in the same direction, just as the effect on total expenditures of the after-tax price of out-of-pocket expenditures consists of two components that work in opposing directions. First, increasing the after-tax price of insured expenditures raises the overall price of health care relative to other goods and services and, thereby, lowers health-care spending. Second, increasing the after-tax price of insured expenditures raises the price of purchasing health care through insurance relative to out of pocket. The second effect induces people to shift to health plans with higher deductibles and coinsurance rates which, in turn, lowers health-care spending as well.

The sign of $e(t_o)$, then, depends on the relative magnitudes of $e(p)$ and $e(t_i)$. The previous literature offers empirical estimates of these two terms. Based on the RAND National Health Insurance Experiment, W. G. Manning and colleagues reported in 1987 that a 1 percent change in the coinsurance rate leads to a 0.2 percent decline in expenditures.[2] In more recent work, Eichner reports that a 1 percent change in the coinsurance rate leads to a 0.7 percent decline in expenditures (average for all employees 1990–92).[3] These are interpretable as arc elasticities $e(p)$ over coinsurance rates in the range of 25–50 percent.

We are unaware of any direct empirical estimates of $e(t_i)$. According to simulations by Feldstein and Friedman, revoking the tax preference for employer-provided insurance would lead to a doubling in the coinsurance rate (from approximately 25 to 50 percent).[4] This finding is consistent with an unpublished estimate by Phelps.[5]

Jack and Sheiner present results from a simulation using different assumptions from Feldstein and Friedman. They find that the effect of revoking the tax preference on coinsurance rates depends crucially on consumers' coefficient of relative risk aversion (CRRA).[6] In particular, the lower the CRRA, the larger the increase in coinsurance rates. At a CRRA of 1.5, revoking the tax preference leads to approximately a doubling of coinsurance rates (a tripling of coinsurance rates at low levels of $e(p)$, a little less than doubling at high levels of $e(p)$); but at a CRRA of 5.0, revoking the tax preference leads to approximately a 50 percent increase in coinsurance rates.[7]

Estimates of individuals' CRRAs vary widely. Kenneth Arrow suggested in 1971 that they should be approximately 1. Other early work suggested 1.5.[8] More recent research in financial economics suggests a CRRA of 2 or more. An unpublished paper by Louis Kaplow shows that individuals' valuations of a statistical life from hedonic labor and housing-market studies generally imply a CRRA of less than 1.[9] A prudent estimate within this range would be 1.5, implying that eliminating the tax preference for employer-provided insurance would lead to an increase in coinsurance rates from approximately 25 to 50 percent.

At $e(p) = -0.45$ (the midpoint of the range of published estimates above), then, revoking the tax preference would lead to a decline in expenditures of 30 percent (= −0.45 x (50 − 25) / 37.5). To translate this into an estimate of $e(t_i)$, we divide 30 percent by the percentage change in the after-tax price of insured expenditures that would result from revoking the tax preference. Assume that revoking the tax preference would raise the after-tax price of insured expenditures by about thirty percentage points. Evaluated at the average after-tax price, this amounts to a 35 percent increase ($= 0.3p_i$ / $((p_i + (p_i - 0.3p_i)) / 2)$, where p_i is the before-tax price of insured expenditures). Thus, a 1 percent increase in the after-tax price of insured expenditures translates into a 0.86 percent decrease in expenditures overall ($= -0.30 / 0.35$).

Based on these calculations, our estimate of $e(t_o)$ is 0.41 ($= -.045 + 0.86$). The above estimates can also be used to calculate the impact of insurance-market reforms on health-care spending. In the text we reported that our insurance-market reforms and restrictions on "any-willing-provider" laws would reduce insurance costs by 7 percent. Since each 1 percent reduction in the after-tax price of insured expenditures increases total expenditures by 0.86 percent, a 7 percent decrease in the price of insured expenditures due to insurance reform would lead to a decline in total expenditures of 1 percent ($= 7$ percent x $(1 - 0.86)$).

The above estimates can also be used to calculate the impact of medical malpractice reforms. In the text we reported that malpractice reform would reduce the price of health care by 3 percent. Since each 1 percent reduction in the overall price of health care increases total expenditures by 0.45 percent, a 3 percent decrease due to malpractice reform would lead to a decline in total expenditures of 1.7 percent ($= 3$ percent x $(1 - 0.45)$).

The combined impact of our policies is to reduce health-care spending by 8.9 percent. Because private spending on personal health-care services, excluding nursing-home care, totaled $601 billion in 2001,[10] inflated to 2004 dollars using the MCPI ($688 billion), our proposals will lower overall health-care spending by approximately $61 billion (= $688 x 0.089).

The combined impact of our policies is not sensitive to our assumptions about the magnitude of $e(p)$, the responsiveness of health expenditures to their overall price. Even if $e(p)$ is half as great as we assume it is, the total effect of our package on health spending is 9.4 percent:

Tax deductibility: $e(t_i) = -0.43$, $e(t_o) = 0.2$, effect on spending = 0.2 x 0.15 = 3 percent.

Insurance reform: effect on spending = 0.07 x (1 − 0.43) = 4 percent.

Malpractice reform: effect on spending = 0.03 x (1 − 0.2) = 2.4 percent.

Appendix B

How Much Must Coinsurance Rates Rise in Order for Spending to Decline by 6 Percent?

As we noted in appendix A, each 1 percent increase in coinsurance rates reduces health-care spending by approximately 0.45 percent. This response is an estimate of what would occur if out-of-pocket spending were not tax deductible. When out-of-pocket spending is tax deductible, individuals will be less responsive to a given increase in the coinsurance rate, because the ability to deduct coinsurance payments attenuates the effect of cost sharing on spending decisions.

Without deductibility, coinsurance rates would have to increase by 14 percent (= 6.2 / 0.45) in order for health spending to decline by 6.2 percent. With deductibility, assuming a tax rate of fourteen percentage points, coinsurance rates would have to increase by 33 percent (= (1.14 / (1 − 0.14)) − 1) in order for health spending to decline by 6.2 percent.

Estimates from previous research also allow us to calculate the impact of tax deductibility on expenditures on health insurance. As discussed in appendix A, eliminating the current health-care tax exclusion would result in a doubling of effective coinsurance rates from approximately twenty-five to fifty percentage points.[1] According to Phelps, that would reduce health-insurance expenditures by 45 percent.[2] The estimate presented above indicated that allowing out-of-pocket expenses to be tax deductible could raise coinsurance rates from twenty-five to thirty-three percentage points. Hence, if an increase in coinsurance rates from twenty-five to fifty percentage points (that is, of 67 percent = $(50 - 25) / ((50 + 25) / 2)$) produces a 45 percent decline in health-insurance expenditures, then an increase from twenty-five to thirty-five percentage points (that is, of 33 percent = $(35 - 25) / ((35 + 25) / 2)$) would produce a reduction of approximately 22 percent in health-insurance expenditures.

Estimating the Impact of Policy Reforms on Uninsurance

To estimate effects of deductibility on the uninsured, we used estimates from Pauly and Herring of the elasticity of insurance takeup by the uninsured with respect to the price.[1] Pauly and Herring estimate that a 25 percent proportional credit would reduce the number of uninsured by between 13.3 and 38.9 percent. This reduction implies an elasticity of insurance takeup with respect to the price of between −0.53 (= 0.133 / 0.25) and −1.56 (= 0.389 / 0.25).

According to calculations using the household-level data in the Medical Expenditure Panel Survey, nearly half (46 percent) of the 43 million nonelderly uninsured individuals are in households earning at least 200 percent of poverty. Assuming that each of these households has both a working member and pays taxes, we estimate that there are about 20 million uninsured who would benefit from tax deductibility.

The impact of tax deductibility on the cost of insurance for these 20 million persons depends upon whether their households have employer-provided insurance, which is currently tax deductible, or whether they acquire insurance in the individual market, which by and large is not tax deductible. For those in the individual market, the effect of the policy on the incentive to buy insurance is especially large because, by purchasing it, a person could deduct both insurance premiums and any out-of-pocket expenses, neither of which is deductible under current law. For example, consider a person who is contemplating the purchase of an insurance plan that costs $1,000 and would leave him with expected out-of-pocket expenses of $1,000. Assuming a marginal tax rate of 15 percent, this person would receive a tax reduction of $300, which translates into a 30 percent reduction in the cost of insurance. For a similar individual who has access to an (already tax-favored) employer-sponsored plan, the effect of the policy is still significant, but it is only 15 percent.

How many uninsured individuals are in each market? Pauly and Herring estimate approximately 60 percent of uninsured workers and their uninsured dependents—or 12 million persons—were not offered insurance by the worker's employer.[2] Hence, these persons are in the individual market.

Assuming a marginal tax rate of 15 percent and a catastrophic insurance policy that has out-of-pocket expenses equal to premiums, full deductibility leads to a reduction in the price of insurance of 30 percent. Thus, the reduction in the uninsured on account of deductibility lies between 2 million (= 12 x 0.30 x 0.53) and 6 million (= 12 x 0.30 x 1.56), depending on the elasticity of the takeup of insurance with respect to the price.

The tax credit will further reduce the number of uninsured. Using the elasticities from Pauly and Herring and the population data in the text, we estimate that a 25 percent proportional credit given to individuals earning less than the poverty threshold (with a linear phaseout from 100 to 300 percent of the poverty threshold) will reduce the number of uninsured by between 2 million (= 43 x 0.21 x 0.25 credit x 0.53 + 43 x 0.47 x 0.25 credit x 0.53 x linear phaseout 0.5) and 7 million (= 43 x 0.21 x 0.25 credit x 1.56 + 43 x 0.47 x 0.25 credit x 1.56 x 0.5 linear phaseout) individuals.

For market and malpractice reforms, we estimate that the total effect of exemption from state mandates and any-willing-provider laws and enhanced competition will be to reduce costs by approximately 7 percent; the effect of malpractice reforms will be to reduce costs by 3 percent. Given the range of elasticities of insurance takeup with respect to the price, we estimate that the insurance-market and malpractice reforms will reduce the number of uninsured by between 2 million (= 43 x 0.53 x (0.07 + 0.03)) and 7 million (= 43 x 1.56 x (0.07 + 0.03)) individuals.

Phelps estimates that a modest insurance policy increases an uninsured person's health spending by 27 percent.[3] Applying this estimate to annual base level of health-care spending by a typical uninsured person, $977,[4] this increase amounts to $264; so we estimate that the credit will increase overall spending by approximately $1 billion (= 5,000,000 x 264).

Derivation of the Elasticity of Total Health-Care Spending with Respect to the After-Tax Price of Out-of-Pocket Spending

Suppose that each individual desires a level of health expenditures E. To reach this level of expenditures, the individual chooses a health-insurance plan that has two parameters, a deductible D and coinsurance rate C. There is a one-to-one mapping between E and (D, C):

$$E = E[D, C].$$

Deductibles and coinsurance rates are each a function of the loading charge (that is, administrative expenses) of insurance ℓ; the tax preference given to insured expenditures τ_i, $\tau_i = (1 - t)$, where t is the combined income- and payroll-tax rate charged on labor income that is not spent on health insurance; the tax preference given to out-of-pocket expenditures τ_o, $\tau_o = 1$ under current law; and the price of health-care services P_c:

$$E = E[D(\ell, \tau_i, \tau_o, P_c), C(\ell, \tau_i, \tau_o, P_c)] = E\left[P_h, \frac{P_o}{P_i}\right],$$

where P_o is the net price of out-of-pocket expenditures and P_i is the net price of insured expenditures:

$$P_o = P_c(1 - \tau_o) = P_c \tau_o$$

$$P_i = P_c(1 - t)(1 - \ell) = P_c \tau_i(1 + \ell)$$

with:

$$\frac{P_o}{P_i} = \frac{\tau_o}{(1 + \ell)\tau_i}$$

and the net price of health care P_h:

$$P_h = \alpha P_i + (1 - \alpha) P_o = [\alpha \tau_i(1 + \ell) + (1 - \alpha) \tau_o] P_c$$

$$\alpha = \alpha(\ell, \tau_i, \tau_o, P_c) = \frac{P_c I}{P_c H} = \begin{array}{l} \text{share of expenses that} \\ \text{are insured.} \end{array}$$

Define the elasticity of expenditures with respect to the tax preference for insurance τ_i as η_{τ_i}:

$$\eta_{\tau_i} = \frac{dE}{d\tau_i} \cdot \frac{\tau_i}{E}$$

and the elasticity of expenditures with respect to the net price of health care P_h, holding constant the relative price of insured versus out-of-pocket expenditures, as η_{P_h}:

$$\eta_{P_h} = \left. \frac{dE}{dP_h} \right|_{P_o/P_i} \cdot \frac{P_h}{E}.$$

Then:

$$\underbrace{\frac{dE}{d\tau_i} \cdot \frac{\tau_i}{E}}_{\eta_{\tau_i}} = \overbrace{\left. \frac{dE}{dP_h} \right|_{P_o/P_i} \cdot \frac{P_h}{E}}^{\eta_{P_h}} \cdot \frac{dP_h}{d\tau_i} \cdot \frac{\tau_i}{P_h} +$$

$$\left. \frac{dE}{d(P_o/P_i)} \right|_{P_h} \cdot \frac{P_o/P_i}{E} \cdot \frac{d(P_o/P_i)}{d\tau_i} \cdot \frac{\tau_i}{P_o/P_i}$$

and

$$\underbrace{\frac{dE}{d\tau_o} \cdot \frac{\tau_o}{E}}_{\eta_{\tau_o}} = \left. \frac{dE}{dP_h} \right|_{P_o/P_i} \cdot \frac{P_h}{E} \cdot \frac{dP_h}{d\tau_o} \cdot \frac{\tau_o}{P_h} +$$

$$\left. \frac{dE}{d(P_o/P_i)} \right|_{P_h} \cdot \frac{P_o/P_i}{E} \cdot \frac{d(P_o/P_i)}{d\tau_o} \cdot \frac{\tau_o}{P_o/P_i}$$

can be rewritten as:

$$\eta_{\tau_o} = -\eta_{\tau_i} + \eta_{P_h} \left[1 + \phi \left(\tau_i \, \alpha_{\tau_i} + \tau_o \, \alpha_{\tau_o} \right) \right],$$

because:

$$\frac{dP_h}{d\tau_i} = \left[\alpha \, (1 + \ell) + \frac{d\alpha}{d\tau_i} \, \tau_i \, (1 + \ell) - \frac{d\alpha}{d\tau_i} \, \tau_o \right] P_c$$

$$\frac{dP_h}{d\tau_i} \cdot \frac{\tau_i}{P_h} = \frac{\tau_i \alpha (1+\ell)}{\tau_i \alpha (1+\ell) + (1-\alpha)\tau_o} + \frac{\alpha_{\tau_i}(\tau_i(1+\ell) - \tau_o)\tau_i}{\tau_i \alpha (1+\ell) + (1-\alpha)\tau_o}; \text{ and}$$

$$\frac{dP_h}{d\tau_o} \cdot \frac{\tau_o}{P_h} = \frac{(1-\ell)\tau_o}{\tau_i \alpha (1+\ell) + (1-\alpha)\tau_o} + \frac{\alpha_{\tau_o}(\tau_i(1+\ell) - \tau_o)\tau_o}{\tau_i \alpha (1+\ell) + (1-\alpha)\tau_o},$$

where:

$$\phi = \frac{\tau_i(1+\ell) - \tau_o}{\tau_i \alpha (1+\ell) + (1-\alpha)\tau_o}.$$

In terms of the elasticity of health-care services with respect to the price η_{P_c}:

$$\eta_{\tau_o} = -\eta_{\tau_i} + \eta_{P_c}\left[\frac{1 + \phi(\tau_i \alpha_{\tau_i} + \tau_o \alpha_{\tau_o})}{1 + \phi P_c \alpha_{P_c}}\right]$$

because:

$$\underbrace{\frac{dE}{dP_c}\bigg|_{P_o/P_i} \cdot \frac{P_c}{E}}_{\eta_{P_c}} = \underbrace{\frac{dE}{dP_h}\bigg|_{P_o/P_i} \cdot \frac{P_h}{E}}_{\eta_{P_h}} \cdot \frac{P_c}{P_h} \cdot \underbrace{\frac{dP_h}{dP_c}\bigg|_{P_o/P_i}}_{\frac{P_h}{P_c} + P_c[\alpha_{P_c}(\tau_i(1+\ell) - \tau_o)]}$$

$$\eta_{P_c} = \eta_{P_h}\left[1 + \frac{\alpha_{P_c}(\tau_i(1+\ell) - \tau_o)P_c}{\alpha\tau_i(1+\ell) + (1-\alpha)\tau_o}\right] = \eta_{P_h}[1 + \phi P_c \alpha_{P_c}].$$

But for reasonable parameter values,

$$\eta_{\tau_o} \cong -\eta_{\tau_i} + \eta_{P_c}.$$

Consider $\ell = 0.2$, $\tau_i = (1- t) = 0.7$, $\tau_o = 1$, and $\alpha = 0.85$; then

$$\phi = \frac{0.7\,(1.2) - 1}{0.85\,(.7)\,(1.2) + .15} = -0.185.$$

Assume the approximate magnitude of $\alpha_{P_c}\, P_c$ is 0.01: if a 10 percent increase in P_c leads to a 0.1 decrease in the share of insured expenditures, then $\alpha_{P_c}\, P_c = 0.01$. Assume the approximate magnitude of $\alpha_{\tau_i}\, \tau_i + \alpha_{\tau_o}\tau_o$ is -0.1: if a 10 percent increase in τ_i and a 10 percent increase in τ_o decreases insured expenditures' share by 0.1, then $\alpha_{\tau_i}\, \tau_i + \alpha_{\tau_o}\tau_o = -0.1$.

In this case, $\dfrac{1 + \phi\,(\tau_i \alpha_{\tau_i} + \tau_o \alpha_{\tau_o})}{1 + \phi\, P_c \alpha_{P_c}} = 1.016$.

Appendix E

Estimating the Impact of Policy Reforms on the Federal Budget

Below, we provide details behind our calculations of the effect on the federal budget of tax deductibility, the tax credit, and insurance-market and malpractice reforms.

Tax Deductibility

Deductibility has two effects on the federal budget: a revenue gain from the shift in health-care spending away from insurance and the reduction in total health-care expenditures, and a revenue loss from making previously taxable expenditures tax deductible.

First, full deductibility will lead to a sizable shift in how medical care is purchased, away from insurance and toward out-of-pocket expenses, and to a considerable net reduction in health-care spending. Earlier, we estimated that tax deductibility would cause private health-insurance expenditures to decline by about 22 percent. Total contributions to employer-provided insurance are about $500 billion in 2004 dollars.[1] Thus, a 22 percent decline in private insurance expenditures equals $110 billion. A portion of this reduction will be channeled into other productive economic activities. Just as increases in health-insurance costs are borne by workers in the form of lower wages, decreases will accrue to them in the form of higher wages. We estimate that deductibility will decrease overall private health-care spending by 6.2 percent, or $43 billion. The remaining $67 billion of health-insurance savings will be shifted to out-of-pocket spending.

The shift in how health care is purchased and the net reduction in health-care spending will significantly affect federal revenue. The $110 billion in health-insurance savings is currently excluded from both income and payroll taxes. The portion of spending through insurance that is shifted to out-of-pocket expenses, $67 billion, will still be exempt from income taxation, but will be subject to a 15 percent payroll-tax rate. This shift will generate $10 billion in additional federal revenues. The portion of spending through insurance that is transferred to other economic activities, $43 billion, will be subject to both forms of taxation. Assuming an average marginal federal income-tax rate of 14 percent and using a 15 percent payroll-tax rate, the transfer of resources will increase revenues by $12 billion. Thus, by changing how health spending is financed and by reducing spending overall, deductibility will increase federal tax revenues by $22 billion.

Second, full deductibility will also impose a revenue loss by making currently taxable health spending deductible. Currently, after-tax payments for health care consist of two components—out-of-pocket payments for the direct purchase of medical care and individual after-tax premium payments for health insurance. According to our calculations from the 2002 Medical Expenditure Panel Survey (inflated to 2004 using the MCPI), total out-of-pocket payments for medical care were $149 billion in 2004 dollars, excluding nursing-home care, nonprescription drugs, and cosmetic surgery. We estimate that $32 billion of this amount was incurred by households in which medical expenses exceeded 7.5 percent of adjusted gross income, and so is currently tax deductible; $117 billion is currently not tax deductible. Applying the weighted average marginal tax rate of 14 percent (which we derived earlier), the revenue loss from making current out-of-pocket direct purchases of care deductible is $17 billion (= $117 x 0.14).

Unfortunately, there is no similar comprehensive public database available to identify the amount of after-tax contributions to health insurance by individuals. According to the *Consumer Expenditure Survey*, health-insurance payments by individuals in 2002 totaled about $131 billion,[2] or, inflated to 2004 dollars using the MCPI, $141 billion. According to the Medical Expenditure Panel Survey,[3] employee contributions for health insurance in the private and public sectors were $101 billion in 2001, or, inflated to 2004 dollars using the MCPI, $114 billion. Approximately $20 billion of each total consists of health-insurance payments by self-employed persons, which are currently tax deductible. (We derive the $20 billion figure by dividing the revenue loss from the self-employment deduction, $4 billion, by an average marginal income-tax rate for the self-employed of 20 percent.) Although neither the Consumer Expenditure Survey nor the Medical Expenditure Panel Survey provides information on the tax treatment of these premiums, a recent study found that about one-half of employee contributions are made on an after-tax basis.[4] Thus, the total amount of after-tax contributions to health insurance by individuals is about $74 billion ($74 = ($114 − 20) / 2 + ($141 − 114)). Applying the weighted average marginal tax rate of 14 percent (which we derived earlier), the total revenue loss from making current out-of-pocket payments for insurance tax-deductible is $11 billion ($74 x 0.14).

The net effect of deductibility on federal revenues is the sum of the revenue gain of $22 billion and the revenue loss of $28 billion, or a revenue loss of $6 billion.

Tax Credit

We estimate the cost of the tax credit as the sum of two components—the cost of the credit for currently insured individuals plus the cost of the credit for newly insured individuals. To estimate the cost of the tax credit for currently insured individuals, we first calculated, using the 2002 Medical Expenditure Panel Survey, the cost of the credit, assuming its value would be $500 for individuals and $1000 for families earning less than the poverty threshold, declining at a rate of 2.5 cents per dollar of income over poverty (approximately a linear phaseout over the 100–300 percent of poverty income range), and that all individuals with insurance would claim the larger of the deduction or the maximum credit to which they were entitled, given their family status. Under these assumptions, the estimated annual budgetary cost of the credit would be $10 billion. However, prior experience with a federal health-insurance credit and a considerable amount of academic research on health credits strongly suggest that the takeup rate for a new health credit would be less than 100 percent. In particular, the General Accounting Office's analysis of the 1991 health-insurance credit found that only 25 percent of the eligible population used the credit.[5] We have assumed a slightly higher takeup rate of 30 percent. Based on this estimate, we estimate the cost of the credit for currently insured indivi-duals to be $3 billion.

To estimate the cost of the credit for newly insured individuals, we first assumed that all 5 million recipients (the midpoint of the range of newly insured individuals due to the credit) were single and received the maximum credit of $500, which yields a revenue cost of $2.5 billion. In the end, we estimate the net cost of the credit for this population to be $2 billion, because recipients of the family credit would be subject to a maximum of less than $500 per person (because the average family has more than two people) and because not all beneficiaries will receive the maximum credit (some will be subject to the phaseout).

The net effect of the tax credit on federal revenue is the sum of these two components, or $5 billion.

Insurance-Market and Malpractice Reforms

We estimate that insurance-market and malpractice reforms will reduce overall health spending by 2.7 percent, or $19 billion. This transfer of health spending to other economic activities will be subject to both income and payroll taxation. Assuming an average marginal federal income-tax rate of 14 percent, and using a 15 percent payroll-tax rate, the reduction in spending due to insurance-market and malpractice reforms will increase revenues by $5 billion.

Notes

Notes to Chapter 1: The Challenge: Obtaining High-Quality, Affordable Health Care

1. Paul Starr, *The Social Transformation of American Medicine* (New York: Basic Books, 1982).

2. Victor R. Fuchs and Harold Sox, "Physicians' Views of the Relative Importance of Thirty Medical Innovations," *Health Affairs* 20 (2001): 30–42.

3. See U.S. Council of Economic Advisers, *Economic Report of the President* (Washington, D.C.: U.S. Government Printing Office, 2002, 2004) for several recent indicators of American preeminence in health technology.

4. "Survey Results on Cost of Health Care and Health Insurance," Market Strategies, Inc.: Livonia, Mich. (2004).

5. The following statistics are from David Cutler and Ellen Meara, "Changes in the Age Distribution of Mortality over the Twentieth Century," in *Perspectives on the Economics of Aging*, ed. David A. Wise (Chicago: University of Chicago Press, 2004).

6. See David M. Cutler and Srikanth Kadiyala, "The Return to Biomedical Research: Treatment and Behavioral Effects," in *Measuring the Gains From Medical Research: An Economic Approach*, ed. Kevin M. Murphy and Robert H. Topel (Chicago: University of Chicago Press, 2003).

7. Mark McClellan and Daniel Kessler, eds., *A Global Analysis of Technological Change in Health Care: Heart Attack* (Ann Arbor: University of Michigan Press, 2002).

8. David M. Cutler, *Your Money or Your Life* (Oxford: Oxford University Press, 2004).

9. All figures are expressed in present value terms.

10. Richard Frank et al., "The Value of Mental Health Care at the System Level: The Case of Treating Depression," *Health Affairs* 18 (1999): 71–88.

11. McClellan and Kessler, *Global Analysis*.

12. Uwe Reinhardt, Peter Hussey, and Gerard Anderson, "U.S. Health Care Spending in an International Context," *Health Affairs* 23 (2004): 10–25.

13. Kaiser Family Foundation, *Employer Health Benefits: Annual Survey Summary of Findings* (Menlo Park, Calif.: Kaiser Family Foundation, 2000, 2003).

14. "Survey Results on Cost of Health Care and Health Insurance," Market Strategies, Inc.

15. See, for example, J. P. Newhouse, "Medical Care Costs: How Much Welfare Loss?" *Journal of Economic Perspectives* 6 (Summer 1992): 3–21.

16. Mark McClellan et al. "Does More Intensive Treatment of Acute Myocardial Infarction in the Elderly Reduce Mortality?" *Journal of the American Medical Association* 272 (1994): 859–66.

17. Frank et al., "The Value of Mental Health Care at the System Level."

18. Martin Feldstein and Bernard Friedman, "Tax Subsidies, the Rational Demand for Insurance, and the Health Care Crisis," *Journal of Public Economics* 7 (1977): 155–78; Paul Ginsburg, "Altering the Tax Treatment of Employment-Based Health Plans," *Milbank Memorial Fund Quarterly* 59 (Spring 1981): 224–55; Amy K. Taylor and Gail R. Wilensky, "The Effect of Tax Policies on Expenditures for Private Health Insurance," in *Market Reforms in Health Insurance*, ed. Jack Meyer (Washington, D.C.: AEI Press, 1983); and Mark Pauly, "Taxation, Health Insurance, and Market Failure in the Medical Economy," *The Journal of Economic Perspectives* 24 (1986): 629–75.

19. J. P. Newhouse and the Insurance Experiment Group, *Free for All? Lessons from the RAND Health Insurance Experiment* (Cambridge, Mass.: Harvard University Press, 1993).

20. U.S. Congress, Congressional Budget Office, *Increasing Small-Firm Health Insurance Coverage through Association Health Plans and Healthmarts* (Washington, D.C.: U.S. Government Printing Office, 2000).

21. Michael Vita, "Regulatory Restrictions on Selective Contracting: An Empirical Analysis of 'Any-Willing-Provider' Regulations," *Journal of Health Economics* 20 (2001): 955–66.

22. Daniel Kessler and Mark McClellan, "Malpractice Law and Health Care Reform: Optimal Liability Policy in an Era of Managed Care," *Journal of Public Economics* 84 (2002): 175–97.

23. Kaiser Family Foundation, *Employer Health Benefits*.

24. U.S. Congress, Congressional Budget Office, *How Many People Lack Health Insurance and for How Long?* (Washington, D.C.: U.S. Government Printing Office, 2003).

25. Jonathan Gruber, "Medicaid," National Bureau of Economic Research, Working Paper No. 7829, August 2000.

26. Dahlia K. Remler, Jason E. Rachlin, and Sherry A. Glied, "What Can the Take-Up of Other Programs Teach Us about How to Improve Take-Up of Health Insurance Programs?" National Bureau of Economic Research, Working Paper No. 8185, 2001.

27. U.S. Bureau of the Census, "Health Insurance Coverage: Consumer Income," by Robert Mills, *Current Population Reports 1999*, No. P60-211 (Washington, D.C.: U.S. Government Printing Office, 2000).

28. U.S. Congress, *How Many People Lack Health Insurance and for How Long?*

29. Blue Cross/Blue Shield Association, *The Uninsured in America* (Washington, D.C.: Blue Cross/Blue Shield Association, 2003); U.S. Bureau of the Census, "Health Insurance Coverage," by Robert Mills and Shailesh Bhandari, *Current Population Reports 2002*, No. P60-223 (Washington, D.C.: U.S. Government Printing Office, 2003).

30. U.S. Bureau of the Census, "Health Insurance Coverage: Consumer Income"; U.S. Bureau of the Census, "Health Insurance Coverage."

31. U.S. Congress, *How Many People Lack Health Insurance and for How Long?*

32. "Survey Results on Cost of Health Care and Health Insurance," Market Strategies, Inc.

33. Robert Blendon et al., "Understanding the Managed Care Backlash," *Health Affairs* 17 (1998): 80–94.

34. For a comprehensive review of studies, see Sherry Glied, "Managed Care," in *Handbook of Health Economics*, ed. A. J. Culyer and J. P. Newhouse, volume 1A (Amsterdam: North-Holland, 2000).

35. Institute of Medicine, *To Err Is Human: Building a Safer Medical System* (Washington D.C.: National Academy Press, 2000).

36. Paul Weiler et al., *A Measure of Malpractice: Medical Injury, Malpractice Litigation, and Patient Compensation* (Cambridge, Mass.: Harvard University Press, 1993).

37. Eric J. Thomas et al., "Incidence and Types of Adverse Events and Negligent Care in Utah and Colorado," *Medical Care* 39 (2000): 261–71.

38. Based on an overall elasticity of demand for health insurance of −1.1 in U.S. Congress, *Increasing Small-Firm Health Insurance Coverage.*

Notes to Chapter 2: Five Policy Reforms to Make Markets Work

1. Melissa A. Thomasson, "The Importance of Group Coverage: How Tax Policy Shaped U.S. Health Insurance," *The American Economic Review* 93 (2003): 1373–85.

2. Joel S. Newman, "The Medical Expense Deduction: A Preliminary Postmortem," *Southern California Law Review* 53 (1979): 787.

3. James W. Colliton, "The Medical Expense Deduction," *Wayne Law Review* 34 (1988): 1307.

4. U.S. Bureau of the Census, "The March CPS Health Insurance Verification Question and Its Effect on Estimates of the Uninsured," by Charles T. Nelson and Robert J. Mills (Washington, D.C.: U.S. Government Printing Office, August 2001).

5. Feldstein and Friedman, "Tax Subsidies," 171; and Charles E. Phelps, *Health Economics*, 2nd edition (Reading, Mass.: Addison-Wesley, 1997), 356.

6. Charles E. Phelps, "Large Scale Tax Reform: The Example of Employer-Paid Health Insurance Premiums," University of Rochester, Working Paper 35, 1986.

7. Authors' calculations.

8. E. B. Keeler, J. L. Buchanan, J. E. Rolph, et al., "The Demand for Episodes of Treatment on the Health Insurance Experiment," Santa Monica, Calif.: The RAND Corporation, Report R-3454-HHS, March 1988. Amounts in text in 1984 dollars. In 2004 dollars (inflated using the CPI), the amounts are equivalent to an increase in deductibles from $364 to $909.

9. Ibid., table 5.3

10. Newhouse, *Free for All.*

11. The Kaiser Family Foundation, *Employer Health Benefits,* reports that the average contribution was $6,656 in 2003.

12. U.S. Department of Labor, Bureau of Labor Statistics, "Health Spending Accounts," by Haneefa Saleem, *Compensation and Working Conditions Online,* 2003, http://www.bls.gov/opub/cwc/cm20031022ar01p1.htm (accessed May 20, 2004).

13. Julie A. Roin, "United They Stand, Divided They Fall: Public Choice Theory and the Tax Code," *Cornell Law Review* 74 (1988): 62.

14. U.S. Department of Labor, Bureau of Labor Statistics, "Health Spending Accounts."

15. Our calculations assume that the new tax deduction would apply to all medical and dental expenses that can currently be deducted under the IRS's minimum 7.5 percent rule.

16. U.S. Council of Economic Advisers, "Health Insurance Credits," 2002, www.whitehouse.gov/cea/HealthCredit_Feb02.wp.pdf (accessed May 20, 2004).

17. Ibid.

18. M. Kate Bundorf and Mark Pauly, "Is Health Insurance Affordable for the Uninsured?" NBER Working Paper 9281, 2002.

19. Susan S. Laudicina, Joan Gardner, and Natasha Stovall, *State Legislative Health Care and Insurance Issues: 2002 Survey of Plans* (Washington, D.C.: Blue Cross/Blue Shield Association, 2002); V. C. Bunce and J. P. Wieske, *Health Insurance Mandates in the States* (Alexandria, Va.: Council for Affordable Health, 2004).

20. Bunce and Wieske, "Health Insurance Mandates."

21. U.S. Congress, Congressional Budget Office, *Increasing Small-Firm Health Insurance Coverage.*

22. Vita, "Regulatory Restrictions on Selective Contracting."

23. Frank Sloan and Christopher J. Conover, "Effects of State Reforms on Health Insurance Coverage of Adults," *Inquiry* 35 (1998): 280–93.

24. H.R. 660, Small Business Health Fairness Act, 108th Congress, passed June 19, 2003.

25. See http://www.whitehouse.gov/omb/pdf/Health.pdf.

26. L. Achman and D. Chollet, *Insuring the Uninsurable: An Overview of State High-Risk Health Insurance Pools* (New York: Commonwealth Fund, 2001).

27. Ibid. For an opposing (although now somewhat out-of-date) view of high-risk pools, see B. B. Zellner, D. K. Haugen, and B. Dowd, "A Study of Minnesota's High-Risk Health Insurance Pool," *Inquiry* 30 (1993): 170–79.

28. Kosali Simon, "The Effect of State Insurance Regulations on Price and Availability of Health Benefits in Small Firms," Michigan State University Working Paper, 2000.

29. Alan Monheit, "Persistence in Health Expenditures in the Short Run: Prevalence and Consequences," *Medical Care* 41 (2003): 53–64.

30. As noted in Marc Berk and Alan Monheit, "The Concentration of Health Care Expenditures, Revisited," *Health Affairs* 20 (2001): 9–18, these proportions have remained relatively stable from the 1970s to the present.

31. M. D. Cabana, C. S. Rand, N. R. Powe, et al., "Why Don't Physicians Follow Clinical Practice Guidelines? A Framework for Improvement," *The Journal of the American Medical Association* 282 (1999): 1458–65; David Dranove, Daniel Kessler, Mark McClellan, and Mark Satterthwaite, "Is More Information Better? The Effects of Report Cards on Health Care Providers," *Journal of Political Economy* 111 (2003): 555–88.

32. Daniel Kessler and Mark McClellan, "Is Hospital Competition Socially Wasteful?" *The Quarterly Journal of Economics* 115 (2000): 577–615.

33. Ibid.

34. Sean Nicholson, "Barriers to Entering Medical Specialties," National Bureau of Economic Research, Working Paper No. 9649, 2003.

35. Daniel Kessler, William Sage, and David Becker, "Impact of Malpractice Reforms on the Supply of Physician Services," *JAMA* 293 (2005): 2618–25; William E. Encinosa and Fred J. Hellinger,

"Have State Caps on Malpractice Awards Increased the Supply of Physicians?" *Health Affairs* Web Exclusive, W5-250, 2005.

36. Kessler and McClellan, "Malpractice Law and Health Care Reform."

37. Susan O. Scheutzow, "State Medical Peer Review: High Cost But No Benefit—Is It Time for a Change?" *American Journal of Law and Medicine* 25 (1999): 7–60; Brian H. Liang, "Risks of Reporting Sentinel Events," *Health Affairs* 19, no. 5 (2000): 112–20.

38. Institute of Medicine, *To Err Is Human.*

39. Kessler and McClellan, "Malpractice Law and Health Care Reform."

40. For an excellent summary of these arguments, see Elizabeth Rolph, Erik Moller, and John E. Rolph, "Arbitration Agreements in Health Care: Myth and Reality," *Law and Contemporary Problems* 60, no. 1 (1997): 153–84.

41. U.S. Congress, Office of Technology Assessment, "Defensive Medicine and Medical Malpractice," OTA-H-602 (Washington, D.C.: U.S. Government Printing Office, 1994).

42. For a description, see ibid.

43. Gary J. Young and Kamal Desai, "Nonprofit Hospital Conversions and Community Benefits: New Evidence from Three States," *Health Affairs* 18 (1999): 146–55.

44. Mark Duggan, "Hospital Market Structure and the Behavior of Not-for-Profit Hospitals," *The RAND Journal of Economics* 33 (2002): 433–46.

45. Kamal Desai, Carol V. Lukas, and Gary J. Young, "Public Hospitals: Privatization and Uncompensated Care," *Health Affairs* 19 (2000): 167–72.

46. Jack Needleman, "Nonprofit to For-Profit Conversions by Hospitals and Health Insurance," *Public Health Reports* 114 (1999): 108–1119; Young and Desai, "Nonprofit Hospital Conversions."

47. Daniel Kessler and Mark McClellan, "The Effects of Hospital Ownership on Medical Productivity," *The RAND Journal of Economics* 22 (2002): 488–506.

48. William M. Gentry and John R. Penrod, "The Tax Benefits of Not-for-Profit Hospitals," in *The Changing Hospital Industry: Comparing Not-for-Profit and For-Profit Institutions*, ed. David M. Cutler (Chicago: University of Chicago Press, 2000).

Notes to Chapter 3: Impacts of Proposals on Health-Care Spending, the Uninsured, the Federal Budget, and the Distribution of Tax Burdens

1. See, for example, William Jack and Louise Sheiner, "Welfare-Improving Health Expenditure Subsidies," *The American Economic Review* 87 (1997): 206–21.

2. Congressional Budget Office, "Increasing Small-Firm Health Insurance Coverage."

3. Vita, "Regulatory Restrictions on Selective Contracting."

4. Matthew Eichner, Mark McClellan, and David Wise, "Insurance or Self-Insurance? Variation, Persistence, and Individual Health Accounts," in *Inquiries in the Economics of Aging*, ed. David A. Wise (Chicago: University of Chicago Press, 1998).

5. Ibid., table 1.1.

6. Monheit, "Persistence in Health Expenditures."

7. Ibid. The greater persistence of expenditures in this study is likely due to the inclusion of elderly and disabled people in the analysis.

8. For example, Christopher Hogan et al., "Medicare Beneficiaries' Cost of Care in the Last Year of Life," *Health Affairs* 20 (2001): 188–95.

9. Alan Garber, Tom MaCurdy, and Mark McClellan, "Diagnosis and Medicare Expenditures at the End of Life," in *Frontiers in the Economics of Aging*, ed. David A. Wise (Chicago: University of Chicago Press, 1998).

10. This estimate lies within the range reported in U.S. Congress, Congressional Budget Office, *Increasing Small-Firm Health Insurance Coverage*, appendix.

11. Mark Pauly, Allison Percy, and Bradley Herring, "Individual versus Job-Based Health Insurance: Weighing the Pros and Cons," *Health Affairs* 18, no. 6 (1999): 28–44.

12. John Sheils and Randall Haught, "The Cost of Tax-Exempt Health Benefits in 2004," *Health Affairs* Web Exclusive, February 25, 2004.

13. Achman and Chollet, *Insuring the Uninsurable*.

14. See U.S. Bureau of the Census, "Health Insurance Coverage," table A-2.

15. $46,520; unpublished data from Anthem, Inc.

Note to Conclusion

1. Milton Friedman, "The Drug War as a Socialist Enterprise," from Arnold S. Trebach and Kevin B. Zeese, ed., *Friedman and Szasz on Liberty and Drugs* (Washington, D.C.: The Drug Policy Foundation, 1992). See also Milton Friedman, keynote address presented at the Fifth International Conference on Drug Policy Reform, Capitol Hill in Washington D.C., on Nov. 16, 1991.

Notes to Appendix A

1. For MEPS, Survey Instruments and Associated Documentation, see http://www.meps.ahcpr.gov/survey.htm, accessed July 7, 2005. For MCPI levels, see http://www.bls.gov/cpi/, accessed July 7, 2005.

2. W. G. Manning et al., "Health Insurance and the Demand for Medical Care: Evidence from a Randomized Experiment," *American Economic Review* 77 (1987): 251–77.

3. Matthew Eichner, "Demand for Medical Care: What People Pay Does Matter," *The American Economic Review* 88, no. 2 (1998): 117–21, table 1.

4. Feldstein and Friedman, "Tax Subsidies."

5. Phelps, "Large Scale Tax Reform."

6. Jack and Sheiner, "Welfare-Improving Health Expenditure Subsidies."

7. Ibid.

8. Kenneth Arrow, *Essays in the Theory of Risk-Bearing* (Chicago: Markham Publishing, 1971); Shlomo Maitel, "Public Goods and Income Distribution: Some Further Results," *Econometrica* 41 (1973): 561–68.

9. Louis Kaplow, "The Value of a Statistical Life and the Coefficient of Relative Risk Aversion," Harvard Law School Working Paper, 2004, http://www.law.harvard.edu/programs/olin_center/papers/pdf/426.pdf (accessed May 20, 2005).

10. U.S. Department of Health and Human Services, Centers for Disease Control and Prevention, National Center for Health Statistics, "Health, United States" (Washington, D.C., U.S. Government Printing Office, 2003), table 116.

Notes to Appendix B

1. Feldstein and Friedman, "Tax Subsidies"; Phelps, "Large Scale Tax Reform."

2. Phelps, *Health Economics.*

Notes to Appendix C

1. Mark Pauly and Bradley Herring, "Expanding Coverage Via Tax Credits: Trade-Offs and Outcomes," *Health Affairs* 20 (2001): 9–26.

2. Mark V. Pauly and Bradley Herring, *Cutting Taxes for Insuring: Options and Effects of Tax Credits for Health Insurance* (Washington, D.C.: AEI Press, 2002), table 1.

3. Phelps, *Health Economics,* 150.

4. See Jack Hadley and John Holahan, "How Much Medical Care Do the Uninsured Use, and Who Pays For It," *Health Affairs* Web Exclusive W3-66, 2003, table 1.

Notes to Appendix E

1. U.S. Department of Health and Human Services, Centers for Disease Control and Prevention, National Center for Health Statistics, "Health, United States," table 120, increased by the MCPI.

2. U.S. Department of Labor, Bureau of Labor Statistics, *Consumer Expenditure Survey Standard Tables* (2002), table 3: Age of Reference Person: Average Annual Expenditures and Characteristics, Consumer Expenditure Survey, 2002, http://www.bls.gov/cex/2002/Standard/age.pdf (accessed May 20, 2004).

3. Agency for Health Care Research and Quality, Medical Expenditure Panel Survey, National Totals for Enrollees and Cost of Health Insurance Coverage for the Private and Public Sectors, 2003, tables IV.A.1. and IV.B.1, http://www.meps.ahrq.gov/MEPS DATA/ic/2001/Tables_IV/TIVA1.pdf and http://www.meps.ahrq .gov/MEPSDATA/ic/2001/Tables_IV/TIVB1.pdf (accessed May 20, 2004).

4. Jonathan Gruber and Ebonya Washington, "Subsidies to Employee Health Insurance Premiums and the Health Insurance Market," NBER Working Paper 9567, 2003.

5. U.S. General Accounting Office, "Health Insurance Tax Credit." GAO/GGD-94-99 (Washington, D.C.: U.S. Government Printing Office, 1994).

About the Authors

John F. Cogan is the Leonard and Shirley Ely Senior Fellow at the Hoover Institution, Stanford University.

R. Glenn Hubbard is the dean and the Russell L. Carson Professor of Finance and Economics, Graduate School of Business, and a professor of economics at Columbia University. He is also a research associate at the National Bureau of Economic Research and a visiting scholar at the American Enterprise Institute.

Daniel P. Kessler is a professor of economics, law, and policy at the Stanford University Graduate School of Business; a senior fellow at the Hoover Institution, Stanford University; and a research associate at the National Bureau of Economic Research.

Index